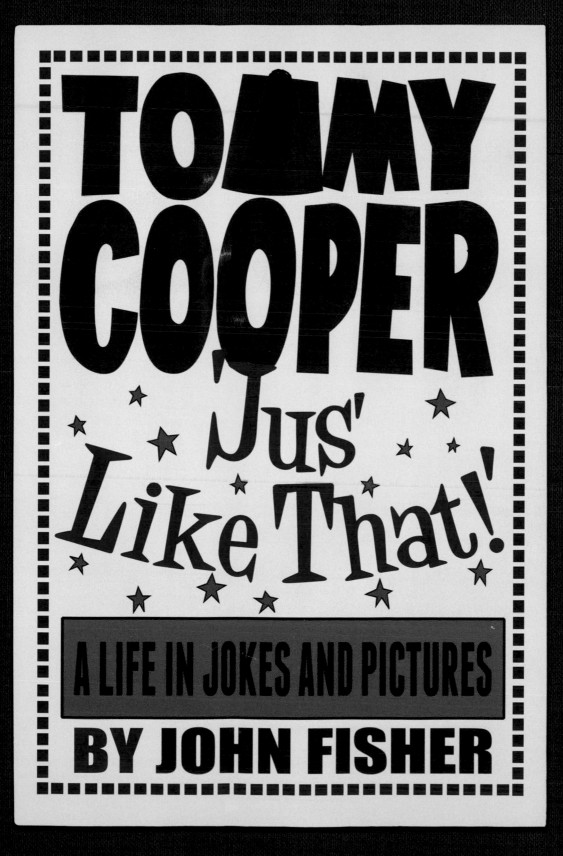

TOMMY COOPER

'Jus' Like That!'

A LIFE IN JOKES AND PICTURES

BY JOHN FISHER

Also by John Fisher

Funny Way to be a Hero
The Magic of Lewis Carroll
Call Them Irreplaceable
George Formby: The Ukulele Man
Never Give a Sucker an Even Break
Paul Daniels & the Story of Magic
Body Magic
Cardini: The Suave Deceiver
Tommy Cooper: Always Leave Them Laughing
Tony Hancock: The Definitive Biography

TOMMY COOPER
`Jus`Like That!`
A Life in Jokes and Pictures

John Fisher

preface

First published in Great Britain in 2012 by Preface Publishing

20 Vauxhall Bridge Road
London, SW1V 2SA

An imprint of The Random House Group Limited

www.randomhouse.co.uk
www.prefacepublishing.co.uk

Addresses for companies within The Random House Group Limited
can be found at www.randomhouse.co.uk

The Random House Group Limited Reg. No. 954009

A CIP catalogue record for this book is available from the British Library

ISBN 978 1 84809 311 9

The Random House Group Limited supports The Forest Stewardship Council (FSC®),
the leading international forest certification organisation. Our books carrying the FSC label
are printed on FSC® certified paper. FSC is the only forest certification scheme endorsed
by the leading environmental organisations, including Greenpeace.

Our paper procurement policy can be found at www.randomhouse.co.uk/environment

Designed & illustrated by Andy Spence Design
www.andyspence.co.uk

Printed and bound in China by C&C Offset Printing Co. Ltd

'Book, scrap! Scrap, book!'
An introduction by John Fisher

I can see and hear him now – in the time-honoured fashion of 'Glass, bottle! Bottle, glass!' – ripping a scrap of paper from a book and then flinging the volume aside with comic disdain – 'Book, scrap! Scrap, book!' To the best of my knowledge Tommy Cooper never kept a scrapbook, but had he done so, this is how I imagine it would have been – a ragbag compendium of family treasures and career trophies, paper memories and comedy moments, all distinctive to the funniest single British comedian of his generation and since. In the process he provides a casual insight into many of his working methods, from the source of his tricks to the meticulous order essential to achieve apparent chaos, from the memory aids for jokes that became second nature to the insight – revealed at an early age – into the character he was portraying.

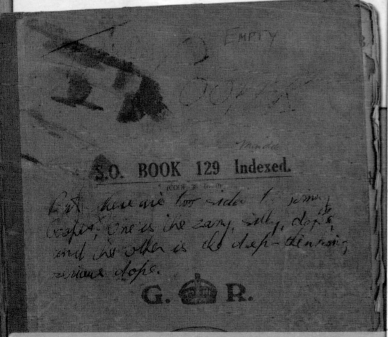

He scribbled the latter on the front cover of a government issue exercise book (more like a desk diary) in which he recorded routines and gags during his time in the services. It reads, 'But there are two sides to Tommy Cooper. One is the zany, silly dope, and the other is the deep-thinking, serious dope.' It would have been impossible to have one without the other. That he concealed the latter from view so adroitly was part of his achievement. Equally instructive is the earliest signed photograph of him I have seen – signed to himself in a moment of cheery self-confidence pre-empting the success that awaited him in the years ahead. I presume the relevant teeth are blacked out for comic effect!

Look closely within these pages and you will also find precise details of the business arrangement that defined his career, an unexpected rap across the knuckles from the Lord Chamberlain's office near the beginning of that career, the record of hidden professional triumphs as far flung as Las Vegas and the Gulf, not to mention surprise documentation of his time in the services in World War Two. However, one facet of this remarkable entertainer leaps off these pages. At the risk of using a cliché, he loved life. He lived for the laughter and the applause and for most – if not all – of the time revelled in the recognition that came from being the most easily identifiable, most impersonated man in Britain. He used to admit with great pride, 'Women come up to me dragging little kids who can't be a day over three. They nudge the kid and say, "Do it. Do it," and then the kiddie says, "Jus' like that!" in exactly my tone of voice. It's incredible and it kills me!'

He never lost his boyhood enthusiasm for the tricks of his trade, while his home became a joke emporium in all but name. His penchant for practical jokes extended to imitation beetles left in the bath, snakes that sprung out of cocoa tins, books that burst into flames or gave out an electric shock when opened. On one occasion he installed a full-size ventriloquist's dummy in the downstairs cloakroom and almost succeeded in giving his daughter a heart attack. One journalist recalled interviewing Tommy at home when a chilling scream reverberated down the stairs. The maid had just discovered a 'severed hand' in the laundry basket. As I wrote in *Always Leave Them Laughing*, my biography of this incorrigible clown, 'He could be as introspective as the next man, but for most of the time to be in his company was to bask in the sun. To walk through the street with him on the cloudiest day was to experience the glow manifested towards him by passers-by, as if a hurdy gurdy were playing and a fun fair lurked around the corner.'

It is common knowledge that towards the end of his days the joy became compromised as his health and domestic life proved victims to the strain of his profession. I prefer to leave this book as a token of the happier times, whether he was sending up his wife in the kitchen, taking pride in his young family, or reducing himself to the level of his kids in the garden. That is how he was and should be remembered. Eric Morecambe, no less, said of him, 'I never met anybody who disliked him as a man,' adding, 'If you didn't like Tommy Cooper, you didn't like comedy.' With his beloved wife Dove to help him keep those outsize feet on the ground, there was no side or pretence to him. If you did not have the privilege of meeting him in his lifetime, I hope that by the time you reach the end of this book, you too, dear reader, will agree.

Tommy was born Thomas Frederick to Thomas Samuel and Gertrude Catherine Cooper in Caerphilly on 19 March 1921. He always claimed that the midwife cast him aside as a weakling at birth: 'She gave up on me. If my mother hadn't kept me alive on drops of brandy and condensed milk, I wouldn't be here now.'

I WAS BORN AT A VERY EARLY AGE – I CRIED JUST LIKE A BABY!

I WAS A SURPRISE TO MY PARENTS. THEY FOUND ME ON THE DOORSTEP. THEY WERE EXPECTING A BOTTLE OF MILK!

WE WERE SO POOR MY MOTHER USED TO BUY ME ONE SHOE AT A TIME!

At various times his father was employed as a coal miner, ice cream vendor, night watchman and poultry farmer.

WHEN I WAS A KID MY FATHER USED TO GIVE ME A PENNY EVERY DAY AND THEN HE'D PAT ME ON THE HEAD. BY THE TIME I WAS FIFTEEN I HAD TWENTY QUID AND A FLAT HEAD!

Tommy.

The family moved twice during his childhood,
first to Exeter when Tommy was three, and
then to Langley just outside Southampton
when he was twelve.

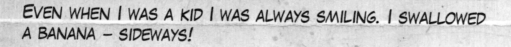

EVEN WHEN I WAS A KID I WAS ALWAYS SMILING. I SWALLOWED
A BANANA – SIDEWAYS!

Tommy left school at fourteen to take up an apprenticeship with the British Power Boat Company at Hythe on Southampton Water. One Christmas, while he was performing a magic act for his mates in the works canteen, the milk that was supposed to stay in the bottle when the bottle was turned upside down gushed to the floor. 'I came off and cried, but five minutes later I could still hear the sound of laughter in my ears and was thinking maybe there's a living to be made here.'

THEN I GREW UP! I HAD TO – WHAT OTHER WAY COULD I GROW?

I SHALL NEVER FORGET MY FATHER SAID TO ME, 'IF YOU GO INTO SHOW BUSINESS AND DISGRACE THE FAMILY, I SHALL DISOWN YOU. I WON'T LEAVE YOU ANY MONEY AT ALL.' AND I SAID, 'I DON'T CARE, DADA.' I DID. 'DADA!' SO HE TRIED TO BRIBE ME. HE BOUGHT ME YACHTS, MOTORCARS, AEROPLANES, A GOLD STUDDED YOYO, AND I SAID, 'DADA.' I SAID, 'I DON'T WANT MATERIAL THINGS. I WANT LOVE AND AFFECTION. GET ME A BLONDE!'

Tommy summed up his potential as a shipbuilder: 'I couldn't even knock a nail in straight.' As war clouds gathered he decided to volunteer for the services. His height made him a natural for the Guards and within a short time his section of the Blues was deployed to North Africa as a reconnaissance unit working with tanks and armoured cars. When he received a gunshot wound in his right arm, Tommy lost his A1 rating, but was given the opportunity of auditioning – successfully – for an army concert party in the Suez area. Note the photo of Tommy relaxing off duty and shots of the desert brought home by him from the war.

I SHALL NEVER FORGET WHEN I FIRST JOINED. THEY SAID TO ME, 'WOULD YOU LIKE A COMMISSION?' I SAID, 'NO – JUST A STRAIGHT SALARY!'

1945

Cairo 20:4:46

1945

EGYPT. 1947

I'LL NEVER FORGET THE WAR. I FOUGHT WITH THE ARMY. IN THE END I GAVE IN AND JOINED!

I GOT THE MILITARY CROSS. MIND YOU, I GOT THE NAVY A BIT ANNOYED AS WELL!

His official Soldier's Release Book reveals that Cooper was no mean trooper!

I ONLY JUST AVOIDED A COURT MARTIAL. I WAS ASSIGNED TO THE OFFICERS' PARTY AND TOLD TO STAND AT THE DOOR AND CALL THE OFFICERS' NAMES!

SOLDIER'S RELEASE BOOK

CLASS "A"

Any person finding this Book is requested to hand it in to any Barracks, Post Office, or Police Station, for transmission to the Under Secretary of State, The War Office, London, S.W.1

This book must be presented at the Post Office whenever you cash a postal draft or one of the drafts in your payment book, to enable the Post Office official to record the date of payment on the inside page of the front cover.

PAGE TWELVE
Army Form X 402

PART I
INSTRUCTIONS TO RELEASED PERSON
TREATMENT AFTER LEAVING MILITARY DISPERSAL UNIT

Under the National Health Insurance Acts, and a medical card telling you how to get treatment will be sent to

an insurance doctor at his surgery, or if your condition requires it, at your home, and free medicine.

had an insurance doctor before you joined up you will be restored to his list if he is still in practice himself or

fill in the application below and hand this book to your previous insurance doctor (or, if absent, his deputy). joined up or if you go to live in another part of the country, apply to any insurance doctor. You can see

doctor will do this.

PART II—To be completed in Unit
Form Med. 50A.

Rank **WS/SGT.** Number **305381**

Initials **T.F.** Surname (Block Letters) **Cooper**

Date of Birth **19·3·21** Sex **MALE** (If a married woman, state maiden name)

The above-named individual left this Military Dispersal Unit on the date in the stamp opposite

Military Dispersal Unit Stamp.
M.D.C.U. and M.D.U.
4 MAY 1947
ALDERSHOT.

RELEASE CERTIFICATE
Army Form X 202/A

Army No. **305381** Present Rank **WS/SGT**

Surname (Block Letters) **COOPER**

Christian Name/s **THOMAS FREDERICK**

Unit, Regt. or Corps **RA/LAA (HQ CSE MELF)**

Date of: *Last enlistment **5·2·39***

*Calling up for military service.
* Strike out whichever is inapplicable.

(a) Trade on enlistment **ARTIST**

(b) Trade courses and trade tests passed

(c) Service Trade

(d) Any other qualification for civilian employment

Military Conduct : *Very good*

Testimonial : *A steady reliable soldier and a good ...*

Release leave expires on **29 JUN 1947**

COMBINED SERVICES ENTERTAINMENT
Unit overseas or U.K. Stamp.

Place **Port Said** Date **21 April 1947**

Officer's Signature

Signature of Soldier **Tommy Cooper**

* Army Education Record (including particulars under (a), (b), (c) and (d) below).
* This Section will not be filled in until the receipt of further War Office Instructions.

(a) Type of course.	(b) Length.	(c) Total hours of Instruction.	(d) Record of achievement.
(i)*			
(ii)*			
(iii)*			
(iv)*			

* Instructors will insert the letter "I" here to indicate that in their case the record refers to courses in which they have acted as Instructors.

Signature of Unit Education Officer

POSITION OF SOLDIER ON TERMINATION OF RELEASE LEAVE

1. A regular soldier with Reserve service to complete will be transferred to the Royal Army Reserve, and will receive Reserve pay until his period of Reserve service has been completed. If on that date the Emergency still exists, he will cease to draw Reserve pay, and will then be transferred to Army Reserve Class "Z" (unpaid).
2. A regular soldier who has completed his Colour and Reserve service engagement will be transferred to Army Reserve Class "Z" (unpaid).
3. All other soldiers will be transferred to Army Reserve Class "Z" or Class "Z" (T).

Notes: SPECIAL NOTE.—Army Reservists are liable to recall to the colours, if necessary, during the remaining period of the Emergency.
(i) Further details of service and of medals to which entitled may be had on application to O/i/c Records, accompanied by the applicant's A.B.64, Part I.
(ii) If this certificate is lost or mislaid, no duplicate can be obtained.
(iii) Any alterations of the particulars given in this certificate may render the holder liable to prosecution under the Seamen's and Soldiers' False Characters Act, 1906.

THE ABOVE-NAMED MAN PROCEEDED ON RELEASE LEAVE ON THE DATE SHOWN IN THE MILITARY DISPERSAL UNIT STAMP OPPOSITE.

N.B.—A certificate showing the date of transfer to the appropriate Army Reserve (A.F. X 202/B) will be issued by the Officer i/c Record Office.

Military Dispersal Unit Stamp.

Society during service, your (See also overleaf.)

re of released individual.)

While still in Egypt after the war he met his future wife, Gwen Henty, a civilian entertainer attached to the Combined Services Entertainment Unit. On Christmas Eve 1946 she found herself accompanying Tommy on piano at a concert in Alexandria. 'I said to him, "Let me see your dots." He didn't know what I meant. I said, "Your music." He said, "Just play the first few bars of 'The Sheik of Araby'."'

WHEN I FIRST MET MY WIFE, EVERY MORNING I TRIED TO BRING HER BREAKFAST IN BED. IT WASN'T EASY ... SHE LIVED AT THE YWCA!

Burlesque Artist Scores In New Show

Beirut, Friday.

Highlight of Ensa show "Sunrise", now playing to large audiences in the Lebenon, is Gwen Henty, who as a burlesque artist, gets right to the hearts of the audience. She has a Gracie Fields personality, her character sketches have 100 per cent. entertainment value, and her vivacious singing at the piano of a charming satire entitled "Men — men — men!" produces roars of laughter.

GWEN Henty (Vicky to you), the girl of many faces, is something of a phenomenon. As the moth-eaten old charlady, she rocks the audience with laughter. As herself a few minutes later, she provokes that peculiar whistle which troops reserve for what they usually describe as a "bit of all right." She more or less runs riot through "Sunrise," the other ENSA show playing round these parts.

SHE SAID, 'TAKE ME IN YOUR ARMS AND WHISPER SOMETHING SOFT AND SWEET.' I SAID, 'CHOCOLATE FUDGE!'

WAS I SURPRISED WHEN SHE PUT HER HEAD ON MY SHOULDER! I DIDN'T KNOW IT CAME OFF!

During his service career he kept up a comprehensive notebook in which he scribbled down routines – some original, some transcribed off the radio – for possible use. These pages reveal details of the double act that he tentatively performed with Gwen when they came back to England. Gwen saw her husband's star potential and wisely decided that he should concentrate on his comedy magic routine.

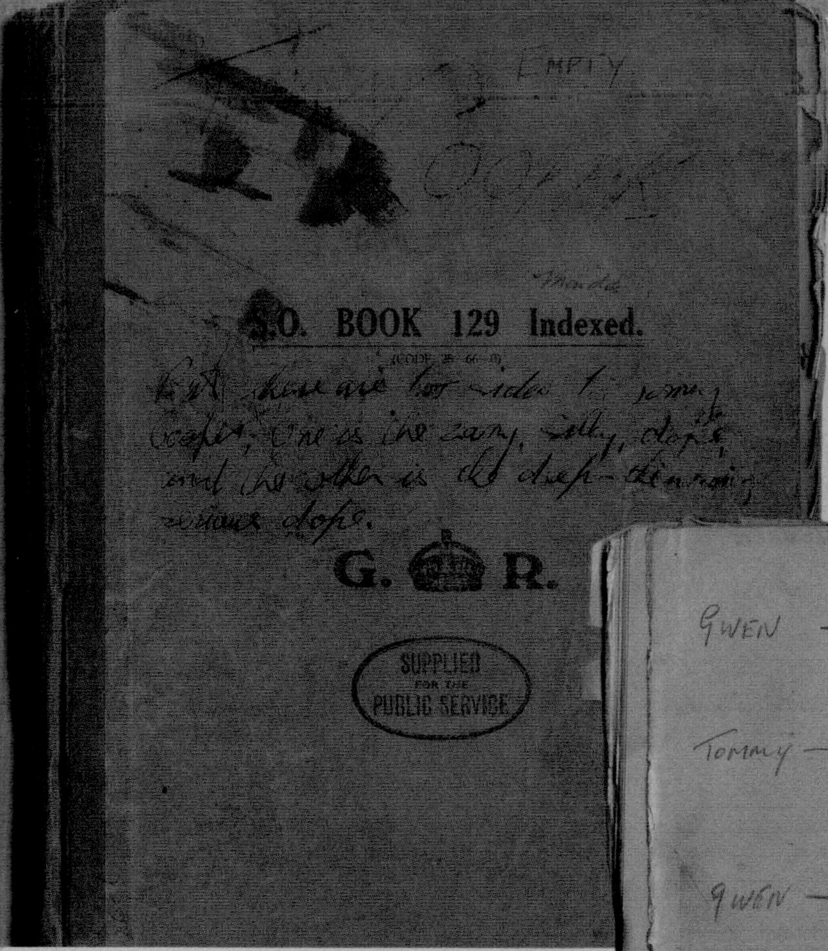

EMPTY

S.O. BOOK 129 Indexed.

But there are two sides to Tommy Cooper; One is the zany, silly, dope, and the other is the deep-thinking serious dope.

G. R.

SUPPLIED FOR THE PUBLIC SERVICE

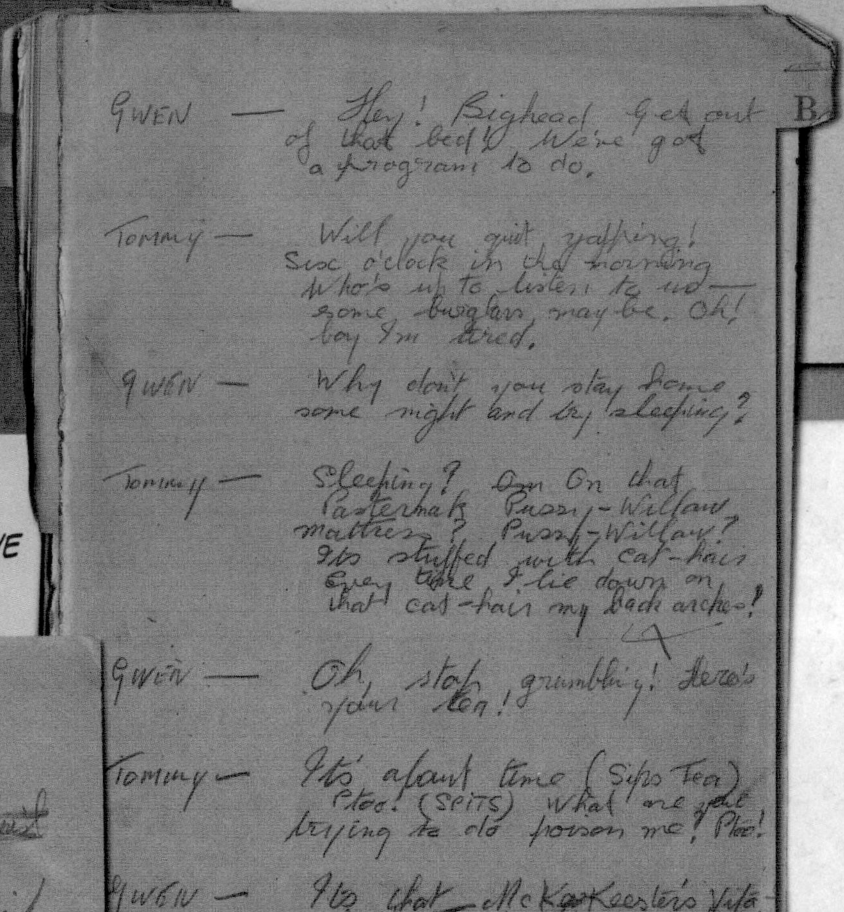

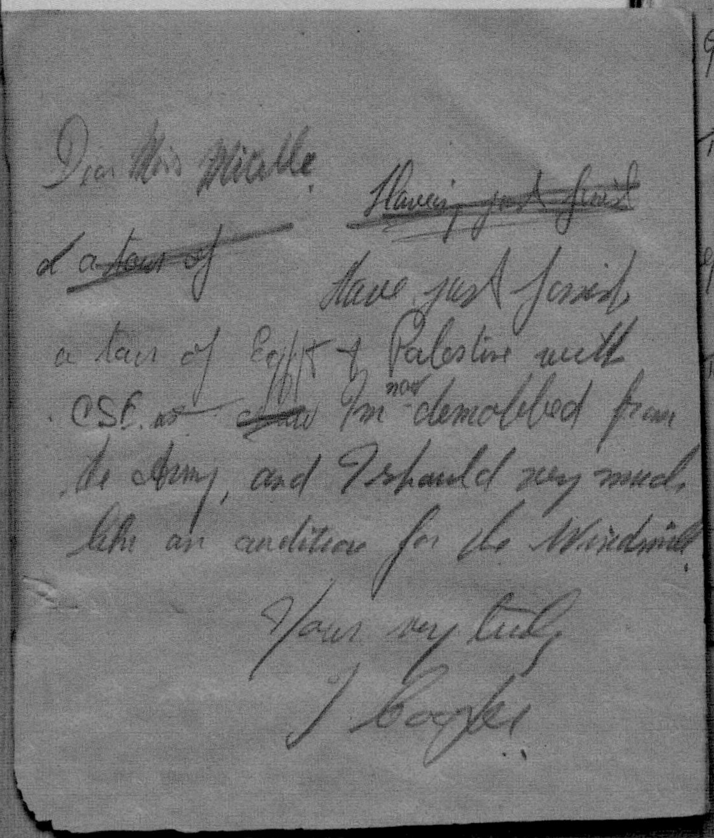

GWEN — Hey! Bighead. Get out of that bed! We're got a program to do.

TOMMY — Will you quit yapping! Six o'clock in the morning. Who's up to listen to us — some burglar, maybe. Oh! boy I'm tired.

GWEN — Why don't you stay home some night and try sleeping?

TOMMY — Sleeping? On On that Pasternak Pussy-Willow mattress? Pussy-Willow? It's stuffed with cat-hair. Every time I lie down on that cat-hair my back arches!

GWEN — Oh, stop grumbling! Here's your tea!

TOMMY — It's about time (Sips Tea) Ptoo! (SPITS) What are you trying to do poison me! Ptoo!

GWEN — It's that McKeester's Vita-Fresh tea! It won't kill you!

TOMMY — It won't? Why do you think the government makes them put that skull and cross bones on the packet? (Tommy screams)

GWEN — What is it?

MY WIFE HAS STOOD BY MY SIDE EVER SINCE WE WERE MARRIED – BUT THEN WE HAVE ONLY ONE CHAIR IN THE HOUSE!

Dear Miss Mialle

~~Having just finish~~

~~a tour of~~

Have just finished a tour of Egypt & Palestine with CSE. as I'm now demobbed from the Army, and I should very much like an audition for the Windmill

Yours very truly

T Cooper

Tommy's draft of a letter requesting an audition for the famous Windmill Theatre. He was successful.

They were married in Nicosia, Cyprus on 24 February 1947 and stayed together until the end of his life in spite of the stresses and strains his profession brought to bear upon the marriage, not to mention the liberties Tommy took onstage with his wife in the name of comedy. He always called her Dove, probably a shortened form of 'lovey-dovey', although as Gwen used to joke, 'Anything less like a dove!' The pictures on this page show the happy couple a few days before the wedding and arriving for the ceremony with their best man and bridesmaid respectively.

I HAD A BRASS BAND AT OUR WEDDING. I PUT IT ON MY WIFE'S FINGER!

I ASKED MY WIFE TO MARRY ME AND BE THE MOTHER OF MY CHILDREN. SHE SAID, 'HOW MANY HAVE YOU GOT?'

SHE WORE HER MOTHER'S WEDDING DRESS. IT WAS A BIT TIGHT – HER MOTHER WAS STILL IN IT!

Upon his return to England Tommy struggled as a comedy magician until he auditioned for his future agent and manager, Miff Ferrie, the resident bandleader and entertainments director at London's Windermere Club at 189 Regent Street. That alliance also endured to the end of Tommy's life, in spite of the love/hate relationship that persisted between the two. Early photos of them and their wives together nevertheless reveal the happy times they shared.

Before becoming a manager and agent Miff had been a successful dance band musician. Born George Ferrie in Edinburgh in 1911, he acquired his stage name in homage to the American trombonist 'Miff' Mole. In the late thirties his presence with his group the Jackdauz on the Arthur Askey radio programme *Band Waggon* brought him national fame. He went on to found his own orchestra, The Ferrymen, and became a popular recording artist.

MIFF FERRIE ORCHESTRAS
(Theatrical, Orchestral & Film Agency)
41 CHARING CROSS ROAD,
LONDON, W.C.2.

SOLE AGENCY AGREEMENT
Adopted by the Council of
THE AGENTS' ASSOCIATION, LIMITED.

To Miff Ferrie Orchestras   Date 28th November, 1948.

Gentlemen,

1. I/we hereby employ you to render your services to me/us as my/our personal representative and manager in the entertainment industry, including my/our appearance in vaudeville, motion pictures, the legitimate theatre, concerts, television and radio broadcasting appearances, private parties or club affairs or phonographic recordings and all other appearances in any wise connected with or pertaining to the said theatrical industry, which shall extend throughout the world and cover a period of...Five years, and you hereby accept such employment and agree to render your services to me/us during and throughout the term hereof.

2. Your duties hereunder are to use all reasonable efforts to procure employment for me/us in the theatrical fields aforementioned and to guide and advise me/us with respect to my/our theatrical career and to act for me/us as Manager and Personal Representative in all matters concerning my/our professional interests whenever you are called upon to so do.

3. As compensation for your services I/we agree to pay you an amount equal to ten per cent. (10%) of all money or other consideration received by me/us during the term hereof, and thereafter, for so long as I/we remain employed or receive compensation under or upon engagements and/or agreements entered into or negotiated during the term hereof, as well as extensions or renewals of such agreements or engagements, also on any engagements or agreements substituted for and/or replacing such prior engagements and/or agreements. Payments shall be due you immediately upon receipt of money or other consideration by me/us.

4. I/we agree that during and throughout the term hereof you shall be my/our sole and exclusive Manager, Agent and Personal Representative and that I/we shall not and will not during said period engage any other person, firm or corporation to act for me/us and I/we shall not myself/ourselves act in such capacity. And I/we further agree that I/we will refer all inquiries and offers for employment for me/us from any other person, firm or corporation to you. You on your part agree that you will negotiate all such inquiries or offers on my/our behalf within your discretion but so as not to prejudice in any way my/our chances of obtaining such employment should I/we desire to accept it notwithstanding that some proportion of your compensation may have been paid to the said other firm, person or corporation.

5. Should I/we at any time during the term hereof fail to obtain a bona fide offer of employment (sufficient to produce for me/us during the time this agreement shall have run a sum not less than the equivalent of my/our average earnings taken over the twelve months immediately preceding the date of this agreement) from a responsible employer in a period in excess of four (4) consecutive months, during all of which time I/we was/were ready, able and willing to accept such employment, either party hereto shall in such event have the right immediately to terminate this contract by a notice in writing to such effect sent to the other party by registered mail, provided, however, that such right shall be deemed waived by me/us, and any exercise thereof by me/us shall be ineffective if, after the expiration of any such four (4) months period and prior to the time I/we attempt to exercise such right, I/we have received an offer of employment from a responsible employer.

6. The period of this agreement may be extended by you from year to year by your giving me/us one month's notice in writing prior to the end of the said period or any extension of that period. Each extension and the determination of such extension shall be governed by the preceding Clause (5) except that the figure of earnings for such extended period shall be based on my/our earnings for the last year of the original period where only one extension takes place, or for the last extended period of one year immediately preceding the new extension, where more than one extension takes place.

7. This agreement shall be interpreted under and pursuant to the existing laws of Great Britain and Northern Ireland. However, should any dispute arise between us, we agree that it shall be submitted to Arbitration. In the case of a variety artiste, the Arbitration Board to consist of one member of the Variety Artistes' Federation, one member of the Agents' Association, with an independent Chairman. Or in the case of a theatrical artiste, one member of the board to be a member of the British Equity, one member of the Agents' Association, with an independent Chairman.

8. This instrument constitutes the entire agreement between us and no statement, promise or inducement made by any party hereto which is not contained herein, shall be binding or valid, and this contract may not be enlarged, modified or altered, except in writing signed by both the parties hereto.

Name of Act, Troupe or Production   TOMMY COOPER

Signed by the Artiste

Permanent Address   13 Barfield Gardens Finchley Rd N.W.6.

Witness

COPYRIGHT OF THE AGENTS' ASSOCIATION, LIMITED
Printed by SEDAN PRESS & P. S. BRAUND, 130, Vallance Road, E.I. BIS 3928.

TOMMY & MIFF 'GAG' (1st routine)

TOMMY..."Well, Miff, what do you think of my magic?

MIFF... "Your Magic ??

TOMMY..."Yes, you know, the way I make things disappear.

MIFF.... "I havn't seen anything disappear.

TOMMY...."You havn't? (Hands wrist watch over).. Yours, I believe.." (then laughs his head off)

MIFF...."Mr. Cooper...

TOMMY...(still laughing) ..."What's that noise ? (looks around) Oh, it's you...What now ?

MIFF....(handing over a pair of sox)..."Yours.. I believe..

(Tommy then pulls up trouser~~xlegx~~ and displays bare legs. Registers consternation, then off (or fade)

....

Same 'gag' (2nd routine).

TOMMY... Well Miff, what do you think of my magic ?

MIFF.... "Your Magic ??

TOMMY.... "Yes. Magic. The way I make things disappear.

MIFF.... "I havn't seen anything disappear..

TOMMY....."You havn't (Hands watch over)... Maybe you'll find this interesting"...(laughs).....(then sinks into chair, still laughing)

MIFF.... "Mr. Cooper....

TOMMY..."What's that noise ?...(looks around)

MIFF..... "Can I interest you in these ? ..(holds up sox).

TOMMY .... Oh, Miff. Don't be silly...Not now..This is no place to.. ...just a minute, let's see....Oh no. Sorry. Not good enough quality...You see, the ones I wear...(lifts up trouser leg. Shows bare legs, registers consternation.)

The combination of comedy and magic – in a more vigorous mix than ever before – made Cooper a natural in Miff's eyes. He signed an exclusive Sole Agency Agreement with Ferrie on 28 November 1948 – initially for five years – and remained legally bound to him until the end of his life. After the five year period Miff had the power to exercise an annual option. However, it was not generally known that Tommy could have walked away if Miff had not sustained the level of Cooper's income as set out in the small print. The personality clash between them was exacerbated by the fact that Miff sadly had no understanding of comedy, although there was little to fault him as a business man. By the seventies Ferrie had made Cooper the highest paid comic in the land and once boasted, 'If the other comedians knew what Tommy gets, they would turn Communist overnight!'

The documents on these pages show the first seeds of stardom being sown by Miff for his client. The 'official' press biography issued by his office provides a handy overview of his early career, even though it gets Tommy's place of birth wrong and falsifies his age by one year. The exposure from his first television series, *It's Magic*, in the spring and early summer of 1952 soon resulted in a better class of booking on the provincial circuits.

PRESS MATTER.

TOMMY COOPER.

Personal Biography: Born Exeter, Devon. Age 31.
                   Army Career : 7 years Horse Guards.
                   Hobbies : Boxing, swimming, ju-jitsu, motoring.
                   Main Interests : Show Business.

Professional Biography. :   Entered the Profession in 1947.
First year fully occupied with Cabaret and several T.V. dates.
(First T.V. date in Dec. 1947, Leslie Henson Christmas Eve Party).

Next 2 years spent touring the smaller Provincial Music Halls
usually doing 'second spot' i.e., the toughest spot on the bill,
a C.S.E. European Tour, a Season at the Windmill (6 shows a day)
and a Pantomime (Ugly Sister) (Learning the hard way !!) Whilst
at the Windmill he doubled Cabaret and in one particular week
actually did no less than 52 shows.

Since then all West End engagements, which have included cabaret
seasons at the Savoy, Berkeley, Washington Hotels, Ciro's, the
Embassy, Colony, Astor, Quaglino's, Churchills, Bagatelle etc.
at all of which he has either been held over or given return
dates. Resident at London Hippodrome for entire run of "Encore
des Folies" from March 1951 till Feb. 1952.

Starred in T.V. series "IT'S MAGIC" every fortnight from March
12th, 1952, till June 18th, 1952.

Debut at the London Palladium July 7th, 1952, when he stole the
show (see Press notices).

August 1952..another Cabaret season at the Colony/Astor whilst
playing London Music Halls.
September 8th, 1952, commenced first Tour of Moss Empires.

Dec. 1952 till March 1953, Cabaret seasons and T.V. appearances.
March, 1953..short Tour on Moss Empires with "Peep Show" Revue
and stole the show again, proving that he is a first class
all round comedian besides being one of the funniest speciality
acts.

Has had the honour of appearing before Royalty at Windsor Castle.

Is booked for the Palladium once again during the Coronation
period from 25th May, 1953.

So far no fewer than 8 offers to appear in the States have been
refused.

Is now firmly established as one of Britain's funniest visual
comedians whose crazy, clean sense of humour appeals to all ages
and nationalities.

....

The man who gave TOMMY COOPER his first chance in December, 1947,
and who has so successfully looked after all his professional
interests since, is MIFF FERRIE, well known in the

Note the amusing throwaway leaflet. It shows that Tommy was never one to miss a trick when it came to publicity.

EXCUSE ME, SIR. HAVE YOU SEEN A TALL GOOD-LOOKING MAN IN EVENING DRESS WEARING A FEZ – I'M LOST!

The CRAZY COMIC CONJURER

from the

Television Show

"ITS MAGIC"

A FEW "MAGIC TRICKS"

—BY—

TOMMY COOPER

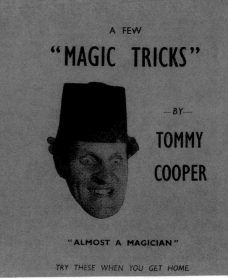

"ALMOST A MAGICIAN"

TRY THESE WHEN YOU GET HOME

A FEW SIMPLE TRICKS BY TOMMY COOPER

THE FLYING HEN

Select a large well-fed hen, the colour is immaterial, though black is the best, and place her in a sitting position on some smooth surface. Then over her place a paste-board box eighteen by thirty inches. Pound smartly upon the top of the box with a bone handled table knife for three minutes, and then raise it, when the hen will immediately fly away. This trick can be performed by any person of average intelligence, who gives his whole mind to it.

THE MAGIC STICK

To do this trick properly you will need a knife and a stout hard wood stick some two inches in length. Sharpen the two ends of the stick and try to crush it endways, either between your hands or by sitting upon it. This to your astonishment you will find impossible to do.

THE NAIL TRICK

Take two wrought-iron nails and wire them in the form of a cross. It will then be impossible to swallow them. There is no deception about this.

THE FOUR JACKS

Get a pack of cards with plain white backs. Take out the four Jacks and burn them before the company letting all see the ashes. Now shuffle the cards quickly, and, holding them in the left hand, give them a sharp rap with the knuckles of the right. Then place the cards on the table with the faces down, and defy the company to find the Jacks, not one can do it.

THE ROPE TRICK

Take a piece of tarred rope about fifteen inches in length, cut it carefully in two with a sharp knife and then try to chew the ends together. You can try this as long as you like.

THE MAGIC EGGS

Put two fresh eggs carefully in a green worsted bag. Swing the bag rapidly round your head, hitting it each time against the door post. Then ask the audience if they will have them boiled, fried or scrambled.

A MAN CAME INTO MY DRESSING ROOM – SMILING HE WAS – AND HE SAID, 'YOU REMEMBER ME?' I SAID, 'YES. IT WAS THE EMPIRE, SUNDERLAND.' HE SAID, 'NO.' I SAID, 'THE PALACE, MANCHESTER?' HE SAID, 'NO.' I SAID, 'THE HIPPODROME, BRISTOL?' HE SAID, 'NO – OF COURSE YOU REMEMBER ME – I'M YOUR BROTHER!'

THERE WAS ONE MAN IN ONE NIGHT. I SAID, 'WHERE ARE YOU GOING?' HE SAID, 'I'M LEAVING.' I SAID, 'I'LL COME WITH YOU. I DON'T WANT TO BE ON MY OWN!'

YOU KNOW I CAN ALWAYS TELL WHETHER AN AUDIENCE IS GOING TO BE GOOD OR BAD. (SNIFFS) GOOD NIGHT!

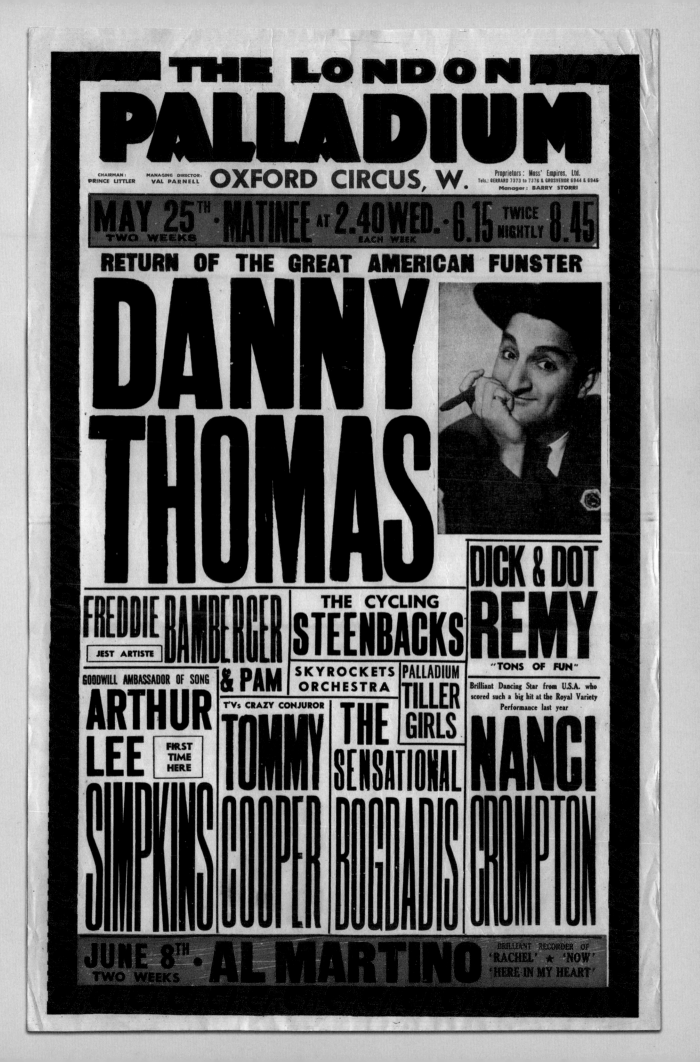

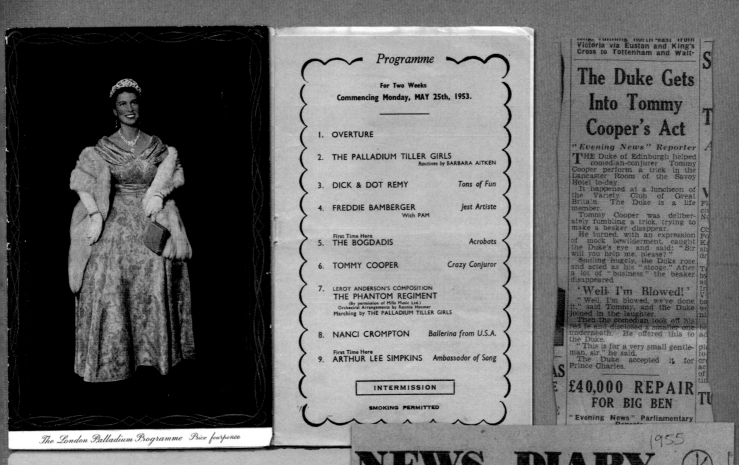

The London Palladium Programme Price fourpence

Programme

For Two Weeks
Commencing Monday, MAY 25th, 1953.

1. OVERTURE

2. THE PALLADIUM TILLER GIRLS
   Routines by BARBARA AITKEN

3. DICK & DOT REMY — *Tons of Fun*

4. FREDDIE BAMBERGER — *Jest Artiste*
   With PAM

   First Time Here
5. THE BOGDADIS — *Acrobats*

6. TOMMY COOPER — *Crazy Conjuror*

7. LEROY ANDERSON'S COMPOSITION
   THE PHANTOM REGIMENT
   (By permission of Mills Music Ltd.)
   Orchestral Arrangements by Ronnie Hanmer
   Marching by THE PALLADIUM TILLER GIRLS

8. NANCI CROMPTON — *Ballerina from U.S.A.*

   First Time Here
9. ARTHUR LEE SIMPKINS — *Ambassador of Song*

INTERMISSION

SMOKING PERMITTED

The Duke Gets Into Tommy Cooper's Act

"Evening News" Reporter

THE Duke of Edinburgh helped comedian-conjurer Tommy Cooper perform a trick in the Lancaster Room of the Savoy Hotel to-day.

It happened at a luncheon of the Variety Club of Great Britain. The Duke is a life member.

Tommy Cooper was deliberately fumbling a trick, trying to make a beaker disappear.

He turned, with an expression of mock bewilderment, caught the Duke's eye and said: "Sir, will you help me, please?"

Smiling hugely, the Duke rose and acted as his "stooge." After a lot of "business" the beaker disappeared.

'Well I'm Blowed!'

"Well, I'm blowed, we've done it," said Tommy, and the Duke joined in the laughter.

Then the comedian took off his red fez and disclosed a smaller one underneath. He offered this to the Duke.

"This is for a very small gentleman, sir," he said.

The Duke accepted it, for Prince Charles.

£40,000 REPAIR FOR BIG BEN

"Evening News" Parliamentary

It was appropriate that Tommy was part of the special bill at the London Palladium at the time of the Coronation in 1953. He quickly became a favourite of the Royal Family and appeared in the first of many Royal Variety Performances at the London Coliseum in November that same year. He invariably stole the show. On one occasion after the performance he infamously inquired of the Queen whether he could ask her something personal. The Queen replied, 'As personal as I'll allow.' Tommy said, 'Well, does your Majesty like football?' She said, 'Not particularly.' And Tommy said, 'Well, could I have your tickets for the Cup Final?'

1955

NEWS DIARY
Evening Papers Broke News to Embassy

The Duke of Edinburgh and Tommy Cooper, TV's "Mad Magician" (left), and Mr. James Carreras at to-day's luncheon of the Variety Club of Great Britain. The Duke had beckoned Tommy Cooper a little earlier to join him for a picture. (See "No fuss—by request.")

No Fuss—by Request

INFORMALITY was the keynote of the Variety Club of Great Britain luncheon at the Savoy Hotel which the DUKE OF EDINBURGH attended to-day.

The Duke, a life-member of the club, had asked specially to be treated as an ordinary member. So instead of the private reception for him he was greeted by MR. C. J. LATTA and MR. JAMES CARRERAS, the Chief Barker, in the crowded ante-room where cocktails and sherry were being served.

New Fashion

Wearing his club tie with its design of red hearts on a blue background, the Duke emphasised his own fashion by keeping the top button of his double-breasted navy blue lounge suit fastened. Until recently most men have left this button casually undone.

Advance instructions from Buckingham Palace told the Press photographers that only two photographs could be permitted. But the Duke, catching sight of TOMMY COOPER, TV's "Mad Magician" wearing his familiar red fez, beckoned him across and told the photographers "please take one more."

For All Ranks

FLYING from Dusseldorf to Paris this afternoon were NAUNTON WAYNE, HY HAZELL, WALTER CRISHAM and THELMA RUBY, principals in the company of "Intimacy at 8.30" which has been playing to British troops in Germany for the past month.

To-morrow in Paris they have an unusual assignment. They have been asked by N A T O to play two days in Fontainebleau, headquarters of the Allied Air Force in Central Europe.

In the 500-seater cinema at A.A.F.H.Q. they will put on their revue (it has been playing to full houses in the West End for nearly a year) before an audience of all ranks.

THE FAMOUS LONDON PALLADIUM — ACE VARIETY THEATRE OF THE WORLD
MAY 25th - 2 WEEKS • MATINEE at 2-40 WED. • 6.15 TWICE NIGHTLY 8.45
RETURN OF THE GREAT AMERICAN FUNSTER!
DANNY THOMAS
NANCI CROMPTON • TOMMY COOPER • ARTHUR LEE SIMPKINS • FREDDIE & PAM BAMBERGER • THE SENSATIONAL BOGDADIS
PLUS USUAL BIG BILL

Tommy's breakthrough in the theatre came with his appearance in the West End deputising for Michael Bentine in the *Folies Bergère* show at the London Hippodrome in July 1950. He had already auditioned for and played the almost obligatory season at the Windmill Theatre, testing ground for many of the rising comedy stars of the day. In the spring of 1951 he was featured in his own right in the second edition of the Parisian revue, *Encore des Folies*.

I SAID 'DOCTOR, I KEEP DREAMING.' HE SAID, 'WHAT'S THAT?' AND I SAID, 'I KEEP DREAMING THESE BEAUTIFUL GIRLS, THESE BEAUTIFUL GIRLS KEEP COMING TOWARDS ME, KEEP COMING TOWARDS ME – I KEEP PUSHING THEM AWAY – THESE BEAUTIFUL GIRLS KEEP COMING TOWARDS ME AND I KEEP PUSHING THEM AWAY, PUSHING THEM AWAY.' HE SAID, 'WHAT DO YOU WANT ME TO DO?' I SAID, 'BREAK MY ARM!'

ENCORE DES FOLIES

Souvenir of the 2nd FOLIES BERGÈRE 2/6

at the LONDON HIPPODROME

The LONDON HIPPODROME

The NEW 1951 FOLIES BERGERE REVUE

PROGRAMME SIXPENCE

THERE WERE SIX CHORUS GIRLS. FIVE MARRIED MILLIONAIRES AND ONE OF THEM MARRIED A POOR MAN. AND DO YOU KNOW SOMETHING? SHE'S THE ONLY ONE WHO'S MISERABLE!

JUST BEFORE THE SHOW THE PRODUCER SAID 'HOW DO YOU FEEL TONIGHT?' I SAID, 'A LITTLE BIT FUNNY.' HE SAID, 'WELL GET OUT THERE BEFORE IT WEARS OFF!'

I'VE GOT SHOW BUSINESS IN MY BLOOD ... I WAS BITTEN BY AN ACTOR!

In subsequent years he co-starred in two similar shows, with Benny Hill in *Paris by Night* in 1955 and with Shirley Bassey in *Blue Magic* in 1959.

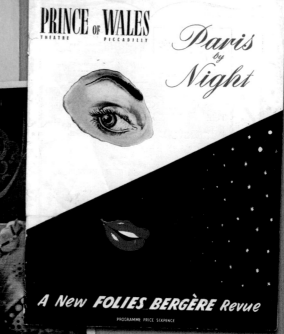

TOMMY COOPER SCRIPT. (Dialogue during comedy magic act)

7 ct. 1951
for Hillsomere

"I would now like to show you 15 hours of magic, and by way of a
change I shall do my first trick first. Now you've all seen that
very famous trick of sawing a lady in half, so to heck with it.
A red silk handkerchief... I will now produce a bowl of goldfish...
What.. no bowl?
Every magician carries a magic wand, ~~I can do anything you like
with this wand...you could tell me what do do with it, and I could
do it.~~ There is a white tip here, and a white tip there. Now the
reason for the white tips is to separate the ends from the centre...
I get worse.. The magic wand clings to my hand..it can't fall down..
because I have my finger there. Wake up fellows, I'm on.
I'll do my encore now while you're still here.. There is the bottle
and here is the glass...the bottle will now change places with the
glass. The tubes are empty. I feel very tired to-night. Been
breathing all day. 'Bush' Bush'! Does'nt mean anything, just looks
good. Music please...That's enough. And the bottle has changed
places with the glass... My next trick..This is called the !Demon
Wonder Box' and was given to me by a very famous Chinese magician
called Hung One. His brother was Hung Too. Box open.. Box empty.
I now produce a blue silk handkerchief, I mean red. ~~See the way I
stand.~~ Well, ~~what if I am.~~ I place the handkerchief in box, say the
magic word 'Hokus Pokus, Fish Bones Choke Us'... That's my best joke.
Okay! and the handkerchief disappears from the box and makes its way
into my left hand pocket...... Please don't applaud, just throw me
cigarettes. Place handkerchief in pocket and produce it from box.
Go home fellows, I'll lock up. The red handkerchief will now change
to blue. In this racket you have to be crazy, otherwise you go nuts!
Yes.. Now'....... We now come to the Bottle and Glass again. Music
please..That's enough. Thought it was a fiver.
This is the egg and this is the bag. You all know what an egg is and
you know what a bag is. I will now make the egg vanish. ... Now I will
make the egg come back. A child of three could do this trick. Wish he
was here now. Where is the egg.... My next trick.. I have 52 cards
here. I will now make sure there are 52. Sorry, 53.
Would you please think of a card? Two of Clubs... Correct!
Will now restore two pieces of rope into one piece... I'm a liar.
I expect you are wondering what this is. So am I.
I can't help laughing. I know what's coming next...
Here is the skull of the magician who gave me that trick.. and here
is the skull of the same magician.. when he was a boy..

Watch! Watch!   and now the Bottle will change places with the Glass
The bottle has changed places. Oh, to heck with it. (Exit).

(Encore) I will produce a bunch of flowers. I wrote that music
myself....(Exit)

In those days all scripts had to be submitted for approval to the Lord Chamberlain.
What was regarded as a frustrating chore to the performer at the time later provided
a detailed record of what constituted his act during his apprentice years. The practice
died out gradually but technically persisted until the Theatres Act was passed in
1968. Here we have an insight into the material used by Tommy at the London
Hippodrome in 1951 and in *Paris by Night* in 1955. Note the lines that were crossed
out – literally blue-pencilled – because they were considered unsuitable for Tommy
in those early days.

Ist spot (Comedy Magic Act).."Good evening..I would now like to show you about ten
hours of magic and for my first trick we have here a white handkerchief
with black spots. I shall now make the spots disappear...There you are,
white handkerchief and there are the spots (Flings them on floor)...
I have here a small piece of rope..for this I shall need the assistance
of a gentleman in the audience. (Flings rope to member of audience in
stalls)...Thank you sir, would you now be so kind as to tie a knot in the
centre of the rope....right...you've done that ??...now tie another, if
you please...and another.... have you done that ?? Good...you may keep
it ..I've been trying to get rid of it for weeks. Now here we have two
rabbits (manufactured) this one is the white rabbit..white hat on box..
and this one is the black rabbit...black hat on box...right...white
rabbit....black rabbit... I shall now make them change places....say the
magic word (gibberish) and the rabbits have now changed places....The
most difficult thing now is to put them back again.... now here we have
an ordinary small frying pan...piece of paper in it...I light the paper..
and what have we ??....just a flash in the pan....Now my next trick is
really mystic...yes ...absolutely mystic...genuinely mystic...and here is
m' stick....and now ...with the help of the boys...I should like to play
a solo on the harmonica...What's it called...Oh yes...."I Get So Lonely"..
.......sorry ..I forgot to take it out of the box....Now we have a tray
with four glasses on a cloth....I shall now whip away the cloth without
disturbing the glasses...I whip it away just like that...or even quicker..
On the count of three...I shall whip the cloth away and the glasses will
remain...One...Two... Two and a Half.....Three....There..I've done it ...
I shall now produce from this Opera Hat a live rabbit...say the Magic Word..
(Gibberish)... It was there.
You have all heard of Houdini, the famous escape king...here is a picture
of him.....he's got away again... Have you seen these...playing cards....
...Here is the white rabbit...and here is the black rabbit...to make them
change places...my next trick... here we have a brass bowl..I now place or
drop three coins in the bowl...One..Two..Three...There you are...three coins
in the Fountain......Oh That Old Black Magic Has Me in its Spell (sings for
few bars unaccompanied) then Honeysuckle Rose (ditto)...(business with
bottles and glasses on table..no dialogue).... Have you seen this record ?
For Square Dancing.... This Magic Wand was given to me by the Magic Circle..
It's the only one of its kind in the world, absolutely priceless (snaps it
over Knee) look at the grain......Here we have the white rabbit...and here is
the black rabbit...see white hat on white rabbit box... black hat on black
rabbit box...now to make them change places....Music please...that's enough.

ADDITIONAL MATERIAL FOR POSSIBLE USE....Here we have a red silk handkerchief.

I will now produce a bowl of goldfish...One two three..a bowl of Goldfish...
What..no bowl?? Well wait till you see my encore..in fact..I'll do it now
while you are still here. Here's the bottle..here's the glass...tube's
empty as you can all see. I will now make the bottle change places with the
glass..Incidentally, I feel very tired tonight...been breathing all day..
Bush Bush wave over it ..Music please...that's enough...and the bottle has...
my next trick...every magician carries a magic wand, and here we have a solid
magic wand, absolutely solid. I will now make this solid wand disappear
before you can say jack robinson...I wonder how Jack is these days... Get a
sheet of newspaper...wrap round the wand...the wand will disappear... get a
sheet of newspaper...disappears before your very eyes...a sheet of newspaper..
look..solid. Here we have a pack of cards...52 cards in the pack..I'll
just make sure there are 52...sorry..53....Would you think of a card, sir ?
don't tell me...just think of it..Now here we have a duck..he will pick
out your chosen card...Now many of you have seen a duck do this before, but
be fair...watch, blindfold...What was your card, sir ? The Ace of Hearts...
Correct....I don't have to do this for a living, you know...I have a big
farm...two thousand head of cattle...no bodies..just heads..   I will now
produce from this empty vase or vause a bouquet of flowers...One, two, three...
a bouquet of flowers...What!
(Alternative) I shall now make this bunch of flowers disappear before your
very eyes.....

(continued overleaf)

2nd spot (Hats routine) ...Here we have a piece of rope...tie a knot in the
middle...like this...see...you then move it anywhere you wish... up
to the top...down here....there...or just take it off... You know..
it's very warm tonight...it's the heat that does it... Now I'd like
to tell you a very funny story...about the three bears...the father
bear...the mother bear ...and the little baby bear...One morning the
father bear comes downstairs and growls..'where's my porridge ??'...
then the little baby bear comes down and squeaks 'where's my porridge ?'.
then the mother bear comes down and says..'I don't know what you're
making all this fuss about..I hav'nt made it yet !!'...And now..I
should like to give you some impressions offamous people of the past,
present and the future.....My first...Uncle Sam...no..John Bull..
Napoleon...right...who's this...Napoleon...O.K. English sailor...
American sailor...two sailors at once....Napoleon....who's this...
oh, not again...We should not have lost the war.... Why??... The
Emperor of Rome...Nero....Napoleon....Get these elephants off the
streets....Buffalo Bill....Nelson....Half Nelson..... It's me all
the time....D'you like the coat...genuine camel hair...yes...real
genuine camel...you don't believe me ?? ...Look.

The second spot for *Paris by Night* featured a routine often billed as
'A Few Impressions', an excuse to don a succession of incongruous
headware that evolved in time into his famous 'Hats' routine.

3rd spot.(Eggs routine) 3 characters. First man..."At this point, ladies and
gentlemen, we were to have presented a real magician, but unfortunately
we cannot, because he is'nt here. However, I myself am a magician, and
I should like to show you a trick which I have performed successfully
all over the world for the last twenty years. In order to perform this
trick, which, as I say, I have done all over the world for the last
twenty years without a single failure, I shall need the assistance of
two members of the audience. Would any two gentlemen care to step on
to the stage ? Any two gentlemen...Ah, here we are, come right up,
gentlemen. (Tommy Cooper, preceded by Ronnie Brody, come through audience
to stage).....And now sir, may I have your hat, there, just hold it in
front of you like this (Brody now holds his hat as directed)...and now
sir, your hat, please (to Tommy Cooper)...Your hat.....may I have your
hat.(eventually snatches bowler from Tommy Cooper's head)... I now
take one egg, break it like this, and pour it into the hat. (breaks egg
into Brody's hat...Cooper starts laughing, till magician breaks egg into
his bowler)...."I will now say the magic word...Abadaba...ABABABA....
T. Cooper ..."You've abadabad in my hat...
First man ....(to Brody)...Is the egg still there...(Brody nods)
then to T. Cooper...Is your egg still there ?
Tommy Cooper..."It's here, but it's not still..
First man... I shall now say the magic formula...Abracadabra etc. Betty
Grable...Betty Grable...Betty Grable......Betty Grable ....BETTY GRABLE..
Tommy Cooper ..."Forget Betty Grable...what about the egg?
First man ...."Is it still there ?
Tommy Cooper..."Don't be silly"

First man.".Ladies and gentleman, after twenty years, I have failed to
do my famous trick...after twenty years all over the world...and now I
have, for the very first time, to admit failure (starts making exit)...
after twenty years ...failed...failed....after twenty years..I HAVE FAILED...(off)
(Tommy Cooper and Ronnie Brody still remain motionless on stage holding
their hats in front of them) eventually Cooper speaks.
Tommy Cooper ...."After twenty years, he had to piekx fail in my hat!!

In his third spot Tommy swapped the role of the magician with that of a member of the audience.
Ronnie Brody, a comedy actor of the day of contrasting stature and haggard appearance, played
his sidekick. The comedy relied almost entirely on Cooper's facial expressions as he reacted to
the misfortune caused to his hat, and his sheer body language as he found himself defenceless on
a stage like so many unsuspecting members of the public in a magician's act before him. The
routine was a clever twist on his standard burlesque. It was often billed in theatre programmes
as 'It Never Fails'. It never did.

The Cooper magic and the inseparable red fez brought fun and much-appreciated colour to gloomy post-war Britain. Tommy's fame soon grew, not least through the coverage extended to him in newspapers and magazines, which continued throughout his career.

That fez on the right is familiar—but who's the up-and-coming magician on the left? We'll let you into a secret—it's Tommy's daughter, Vicky. Her special trick is waking Mum and Dad in the middle of the night

February 3, 1956   TV TIMES   7

HIS FEZ IS HIS FORTUNE

"I took up magic as a hobby when I was nine," he told me in his dressing-room at a West End theatre. "An aunt gave me some tricks for a present."

Off-stage he is not much different from his professional self. The maniacal laugh, nervous mannerisms and sense of humour are still there.

His apprentice days explain what he is like. "I used to show the other boys tricks and make them laugh," he recalls. "If you got into trouble you were sent home. I was always being sent home."

The war interrupted his training and the first few weeks of September 1939 found him learning to ride a horse as a trooper in the Horse Guards.

One of his chores was sentry duty in Whitehall. "I've done that many times," he says. "Khaki uniform though—nothing fancy."

You might also have seen him riding. Army fashion, in Rotten Row at 6.30 a.m.—that is riding one horse and leading two others.

He served for seven years. Four were spent in the Middle East where he was promoted sergeant and developed a passion for hot climates.

How did Sergeant Cooper drift into the entertainment world? He did it like so many others in uniform. He began by making...

following on TV and performed before the Royal Family.

Yet, as one of his friends remarks, despite his successes he does not realise how high he has risen in his profession. Or how much further he can go.

This conversation gives a guide to that part of his make-up. "Associated TeleVision asked me to do a series of six *Saturday Showtime* programmes," he says.

"You accepted?"

"No. I asked if they would change it to three shows to take place once a fortnight. I don't want the viewers to get sick of seeing me."

So there is a gap of a fortnight between his ITV shows.

He took care not to outstay his welcome in America. Last year he went with a British company to the Flamingo Hotel in Las Vegas.

The American Press described him as "the highspot of the show" and other offers arrived. They were turned down because of prior commitments in England.

He would like to cross the Atlantic again to do some TV work. That will have to wait. His current stage show has run since April and his wife wants to know when they are going on a honeymoon...

THINK of any popular comedian and the chances are that the man you have in mind is less than average size.

He wins his laughs by symbolising all the little men of the world—trying to become more important than they are, constantly being buffeted by life, and nearly submerged by trouble.

That is where Tommy Cooper, who made the first of three appearances as guest star in *Saturday Showtime* last week, differs from the rest.

It would take a major catastrophe to submerge... his size... protecting... Cooper... and Askey... than life, w...

being cut de... a trick, co... dissolves in... it fails. An... he deflates.

IS HE THE SAME AT HOME?

Viewers often ask that question about Tommy Cooper, television's crazy comedian. These TV MIRROR pictures suggest that the answer is YES!

... it falls to the floor and smashes. Save washing-up, but Mrs. Cooper doesn't approve. "What are you—you mad?" The saucer's not the only thing that's cracked."

Tommy's favourite disappearing trick. He says it goes down well in any home. For an encore he follows it with mash

December 19th, 1953   T.V. FUN

IN TOWN TO TALK TO YOU

TOMMY COOPER ... The Crazy Conjurer, is specially interviewed for T.V. FUN Readers by our star-reporter, AMANDA.

HE calls himself "almost a magician"—for his tricks never quite come off. His name is Tommy Cooper, the six-feet-four comic who started off as a straight conjurer and became, instead, one of the biggest laugh-raisers on television. I thought you would all like to know more about this...

Tommy, seating himself and beginning to remove his make-up. "When I was a youngster someone presented me with a boy's conjurer's set. I rapidly became interested about making a living... tricks went... You know... under some... and and the... ake." ... and a cup of... rousers... for YOU,...

ly. "I did ... njurer after ... I worked ... body seemed ... should have ... ny tricks all ... ork miracles ... n amateur ... ess of a trick ... er—and enjoy

Miff Ferrie immediately saw the possibilities of a new act—and you can imagine my surprise when he told me that I'd got the job. Always fluff your tricks like that," he said, to my utter astonishment. "I like them better that way."

"I'll remember that, Tommy," I said, with a smile. "The next time I make a hash of something I'll know it may be good luck in disguise."

"I went on tour, under my present title of 'Almost a Magician,'" Tommy told me. "I visited all the smaller provincial theatres and gained a lot of valuable experience. Eventually, I reached the Windmill Theatre. What with cabaret...

WIN £11,500

Go for the great Evening News £11,500 Jackpot Contest. This fantastic money prize must be won!

If there is a tie this huge jackpot will be shared among those tying.

Remember, you and the whole family can enter. Don't miss your chance.

WHAT TO DO Look at the picture of Tommy Cooper, then read the ten characteristics associated with him. Decide which six characteristics you consider show most clearly in this picture. Put your selections in order of prominence from this point of view by printing their identity letters in the appropriate spaces in the first column on the entry form below. You may complete all 14 columns for 21p. Minimum entry is 2 lines—3p. Use ink or ballpoint pen only.

A postal order or cheque must be sent for any amount over 41p made payable to the Evening News and crossed /& Co./. All late entries should be sent by First-class post. No competitor may send in more than two coupons cut from the Evening News.

Full rules may be obtained from "Rules," Jackpot Contest, Evening News, Temple House, Temple Avenue, London, E.C.4.

Result next Saturday.

Pictures selected by the well-known artist John Spencer Churchill.

SELECT SIX

A. Lightheartedness
B. Tolerance
C. Composure
D. Geniality
E. Self possession
H. Vitality
J. Determination
K. Candour
L. Sense of humour
N. Perception

TOMMY COOPER
Mirth making comedian of stage and TV

---- CUT HERE ----

Post your entry to: JACKPOT CONTEST No. 15, EVENING NEWS, HARMSWORTH HOUSE, LONDON, EC4X 1AS (Comp.).

I submit ___ entries for which
I enclose PO value ___

PO number (or stamps to the value of 41p ONLY)

I agree to abide by the rules

NAME (Mr. Mrs. or Miss Block letters)

ADDRESS

	3p	11p	6p	11p	11p	11p	11p	11p	11p	11p	11p	11p	11p
1													
2													
3													
4													
5													
6													

Enter six selections in a downward line: 2 lines 3p; 4 lines 6p; 12 lines 18p; 14 lines 21p   **B**

---- CUT HERE ----
ENTRIES MUST BE RECEIVED BY FIRST POST WEDNESDAY OCT 20

A FEW OF US WAKE UP AND FIND OURSELVES FAMOUS. MOST OF US WAKE UP AND FIND WE'RE HALF AN HOUR LATE!

STARS at the Savoy yesterday: Max Bygraves, Tommy Cooper and Arthur Askey. **Picture: STEVE MARKESON**

WE wanna tell you a story, playmates ... just like that, that and that.

Comedians Max Bygraves, Tommy Cooper and Arthur Askey are pictured yesterday at London's Savoy Hotel—when showbusiness made it a magic day for Tommy.

There were 250 guests at a Variety Club lunch to celebrate Tommy's 30 years of laughter-making.

Tributes were paid to the inimitable Tommy. Not just to the public face under the famous fez but also to the "Uncle Tommy" who conjures up Christmas toys for handicapped children.

The stars presented Tommy with a solid silver tray. Max Bygraves said: "We could not give him the gift we wanted ... how do you gift-wrap a brewery?"

Picture: STEVE MARKESON

JUST LIKE THAT, THAT AND THAT!

DOCTOR! DOCTOR!

Tommy Cooper
Doctor Jokesmith

Jokes epidemic brings rash of giggles

QUICK — send for the doctor. We're drowning in a sea of postcards! We received thousands of entries for our Tommy Cooper Write a Gag competition and below we print the first selection. Each of these readers will be paid £3. The winning joke, which wins £20 plus a Tommy Cooper Fez and magic wand, will be published next week with another selection of gags. We asked for original jokes but great minds obviously think alike: For dozens, hit the same theme (Sample: Doctor! Doctor! I'm turning into a spoon. Answer: Sit down and don't stir). Even so, what a giggle!

Doctor! Doctor! What do you suggest for a hammer toe?
Grow a two-inch nail!
Mrs. D. Wakelam, Smethwick, West Midlands.

Doctor! Doctor! Every time I say "abracadabra," people disappear.
Doctor! Doctor! Where have you gone?
S.J. House, Harlow, Essex.

Doctor! Doctor! What can you give me for big feet?
Big boots.
Frank Wright, Ware.

Doctor! Doctor! I think I'm turning into a TV set.
Keep still man. I'm trying to watch Kojak.
Stephen Smith, Wednesfield, Wolverhampton.

The Fiend in Tommy Cooper

SEE HIM IN "COOPER'S CAPERS", ITV, FRIDAY 10.15

PICTURES AND STORY BY BOB COLLINS

THIRTY-FOUR-YEARS old, three storeys, six feet four inches, extravagant work-on-the-view, Tommy Cooper looped horrily at me from behind the long standard...

Clean humour

Hypnotic pictures

TELEQUIZ

ANSWERS

COOPER COMEDY COSTS A PACKET

SUN TV By PHILIP PHILLIPS

TOMMY COOPER returns to television tonight for his first appearance on our screens for more than three years.

In all that time, hardly a month passed without somebody asking me: "Where is Tommy? Why don't we see him on TV?"

LURE

SURPRISE

WHAT A CARD!

Britain's showbiz showcase presented by **DOUGLAS MARLBOROUGH**

SCENE IN TITBITS

Page 34 TITBITS   TITBITS Page 35

EAR, JUST LIKE THAT!

LET'S hear it for the man with the big ears. Tommy Cooper is back in business — just like that.

The 55-year-old comedian is returning to TV less than three months after being struck down by a heart attack.

Tommy collapsed as he was about to go on stage in Rome. And, at the time, he didn't think it was very funny. But now he's feeling fine and up to his old tricks again.

Which accounts for these antics yesterday as Tommy will wear them in a Thames TV show next week — grinning, no doubt, from ear to ear. Picture: MIKE MALONEY

TOMMY COOPER SAMPLES A TV WARDROBE....

... and DOREEN CHALLIS finds it could provide—

A FANCY DRESS FOR EVERYONE IN BRIGHTON

Comedian hopes to trace birthplace

COMEDIAN TOMMY Cooper returned to Caerphilly last night anxious to trace the house where he was born.

Mr. Cooper, aged 50, left the town when he was a year old and went back yesterday for the first time.

"I would like to see the house where I was born," he said. "I have no idea where it is, but I shall try to find it while I am here.

"I also believe I may have some relatives in the town, and I would like to meet them."

His manager, Mr. Miff Ferrie,

received a letter recently from a resident in Caerphilly who said he was living in the house where the comedian was born.

Mr. Cooper hopes that person will visit the Club Double Diamond, Caerphilly, where he is appearing this week, and offer to show him the house.

When the comedian arrived at the club, he was presented with a portrait of himself painted by a fan, Mr. Walter Hazell, of Boverton Brook, Llantwit Major.

"It is a very nice gesture and a good likeness," said Mr. Cooper. "I shall hang it in the study of my Chiswick home."

Miff Ferrie

DURRANT'S PRESS CUTTINGS
20–39, Mount Pleasant, London, W.C.1.
Telephone: CENTRAL 3149 (Two Lines).

Radio Times
The Grammar School, Scarle Road, Wembley.

Cutting from issue dated.................... 8 MAR 1952

12 Mar T.V.

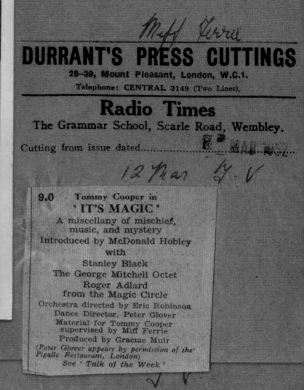

9.0   **Tommy Cooper** in
'**IT'S MAGIC**'
A miscellany of mischief,
music, and mystery
Introduced by McDonald Hobley
with
Stanley Black
The George Mitchell Octet
Roger Adlard
from the Magic Circle
Orchestra directed by Eric Robinson
Dance Director, Peter Glover
Material for Tommy Cooper
supervised by Miff Ferrie
Produced by Graeme Muir
(*Peter Glover appears by permission of the*
Pigalle Restaurant, London)
See ' Talk of the Week '

Cooper made his television debut on Christmas Eve
1947 in a programme starring the musical comedy star
Leslie Henson, although he did not properly register
in the medium until he stole the show from names like
Arthur Askey, Frankie Howerd and Norman Wisdom
on the BBC Christmas Party of 1952. The number of
television sets was now fast approaching one and a half
million and there was only one channel to choose from.
Tommy would have had to play to capacity at the
London Palladium for several years to have gained the
live audience that saw him magically passing a block
of wood – from ear to ear – through the head of
compère Macdonald Hobley (seen above).

'Almost a Magician'

HE calls himself 'almost a magician' for his tricks
never quite come off. His name, as most viewers will
guess, is Tommy Cooper, the six-foot-four comic who
starts his first series of television programmes on Wednesday. Their title is *It's Magic* and that covers a great
many things. As Graeme Muir the producer puts it, ' We
may range from the magic in a pianist's fingers to the
magic of television itself.'
Cooper was born in Devon twenty-nine years ago. He
served for seven years in the Horse Guards and entered
show business in 1947. When Miff Ferrie auditioned
him for a London night club he turned up as an impressionist. Ferrie liked him enough to send him away
to work out another act. He returned in a week and, in
Ferrie's words, ' even made the orchestra laugh.' Since
then Cooper has been on the halls, at the Windmill
Theatre, in pantomime, almost continuously in cabaret,
and at the London Hippodrome throughout the eleven-
month run of *Encore des Folies*.

*   *   *

Full **CHANNEL 9** programmes Feb 5–Feb 11.   No. 20   4ᴰ
TV TIMES

TOMMY COOPER
–Page Three

BRITAIN'S BRIGHTEST WEEKLY   4½ᵈ EVERY WEDNESDAY
TV mirror
AND
DISC NEWS

THE FIEND IN
TOMMY COOPER

TELEVISION HAS OPENED UP A WHOLE NEW FIELD OF UNEMPLOYMENT FOR ME!

TV mirror

March 6th, 1954 Vol. 2 No. 10

4ᴰ
Every Wednesday

MEN OF HOLME MOSS

Exclusive pictures and story

★

RICHARD AFTON'S DIARY

★

Sally Barnes
Karen Greer
Joan Gilbert

★

TV's Travelling Eye

★

Programme Highlights

Tommy Cooper
See page 13

EVERYBODY'S SAYING TELEVISION IS HERE TO STAY. I DON'T KNOW. THE HIRE PURCHASE COMPANY IS TAKING MINE BACK TOMORROW!

A serious student of comedy and humour throughout his career, Cooper kept comprehensive files of every gag he ever told, and hundreds he never got round to delivering, many of them written out in long hand to help in the learning process.

Gags, etc

The first prize will be a free extraction of a tooth of your own choice!!

300 lb, of putty for each member of your family or 4,000 yards of Dental Floss – Almost New!

We were so poor in our street we were the only family in our street with a wind-up television set!

Jack and Jill, Went up the hill, The last I heard They're up there still!!

She had her face a face lift, and when she saw the doctor's bill it fell down again!!

Making Woopie:- Another bride, another groom – I hope they find, a hotel room!!

Show me a man with 2 feet on the ground and I'll show you a man who can't take off his trousers!

Show me a milkman with high heel shoes and I'll show you a Dairy Queen!!

Wish I had a polaroid camera so
that I could get a close up of that
joke dying

When she cooks you get a lump in
your throat - in your stomach - your
arms - your legs.

Show me a man who can keep
both feet on the ground - and
I'll show you a man who can't
take his trousers off

Hotel - 3 o'clock in morning
- Man loses his temper. Banging
on door - What did you do?
Nothing - I just kept on playing
my drums

I'd like to say something funny
but I don't like to break
the spell.

I took her to a restaurant, she said she wasn't hungry
so she ordered a side dish; a side of beef.

She watches so many mystery programs on T.V. that
when she turns off the set, she wipes her finger
prints of the dial.

She used to keep getting headaches, and I kept
telling her, that she's got to jump out of bed
feet first.

I took her to a dance, and she was the prettiest
girl on the floor, I can see her now - laying
there.

He used to get us out for Role-call, and it was pitch
black, and the Sgt had a lamp in his hand. he said
"morning men" and we said "good morning lamp," we
couldn't see him

Opening :- Top up title into - You should
I got a car for my wife, yesterday,
- not a bad swop! I was driving the
other day, and a Police car, pulled me
up - I said what have I done? - He
said, nothing - but your wife fell
out of your car two miles back! -
- I said thank goodness I thought
I'd gone stone deaf !!!

When I was 2 my parents was old
moved. I found them when I was four.
I was born with a silver knife
in my mouth. My father was a
sword swallower! My father gave
me a musical background. He
used to hit me with a violin!
I was six years old when I discovered
I was full of music - I swallowed
a mouthorgan !! I decided to
become an Inventor! For my first
experiment I crossed a mule with a
cow & I got milk with a kick in it.

Quick Short Stories

Agent :- To manager, I've got a girl
who wears a size 102 Bra! The
manager said - Ho one H. and two
size Brassiere? What does she do?
and the agent said - She tries to stand
up!!
A drunk staggers out of a Pub - and
just made it to the parking meter. -
He put a sixpence in the meter and
hung on for dear life, when a policeman
walked over and said - Come on get
going, move along - and the drunk said
Not yet, - I still got 20 m. left!

Photographed on board.
RMS. QUEEN ELIZABETH

Tommy set sail on the first of several trips to the USA on 31 March 1954. The press singled him out as 'the high spot' of the revue *Piccadilly Revels* at the Flamingo Hotel in Las Vegas, the nominal star of which was Vera Lynn, seen here on the journey across with Tommy, Miff and her husband. When the show folded after two weeks, Cooper was not short of offers to continue in America – including one for a season at New York's prestigious Radio City Music Hall – but had to return to fulfil previous commitments in England. Ballantine was an American magician who also performed a crazy conjuring act, although he never achieved the legendary status in his own country that Tommy achieved in the UK and beyond.

Licensed Annually by the L.C.C.

MIFF FERRIE
ORCHESTRAS
(Theatrical, Cabaret, Films Radio, & T.V. Direction)

Telephones
WELbeck 0738/9
Grams. "Emmeff." Wesdo, London.
Cables. "Emmeff." London.

25, DURWESTON COURT,
York Street, London, W.1

23rd March, 1954.

T. Cooper, Esq.,
2, Waverley Mansions,
Kenton Street,
W.C.1.

Dear Tommy,

   Further to our telephone conversation of to-day, please find enclosed herewith your Passport and contract for Las Vegas which you will possibly require to have with you when seeing your Bank Manager re your dollar allowance.

   Please return the contract here when you have settled this.

   Yours sincerely,

   MIFF FERRIE.

2

DESCRIPTION-SIGNALEMENT

	Bearer–Titulaire	★Wife–Femme
Profession) Profession	ARTIST	
Place and date of birth Lieu et date de naissance	CAERPHILLY, WALES 19th March 1921	
Residence Résidence	ENGLAND	
Height Taille	6 ft 3 in.	ft in.
Colour of eyes Couleur des yeux	BLUE	
Colour of hair Couleur des cheveux	BROWN	
Special peculiarities Signes particuliers		

★CHILDREN–ENFANTS

Name–Nom   Date of birth–Date de naissance   Sex–Sexe

Signature of Bearer
Signature du Titulaire

Signature of Wife
Signature de sa Femme

EEN 7000 696
PHOTOGRAPH OF BEARER

WIFE   FEMME

(photo)

3

Transportation from London to Las Vegas and back.

By sea. Southampton to New York   Cost for 2 people.
Queen Elizabeth sailing March 31st
2 single cabins(B.145 &147) at £145 each............ £ 290. 0. 0.

By rail. New York to Las Vegas
(Double room for 2 people)......................... 81. 1. 9.
(Meals on train will be extra)

Cost of outward journey by above means of travel   £ 371. 1. 9.

Return by air from Las Vegas to London
              (via Los Angeles)

1st Class ..£205. 5. 0. each
              (sleeper £12. 10. 0. extra)

Tourist Class.. £140. 7. 0. each..................... 280. 14. 0.

World's Tallest

Photo Made Atop Empire State Building, New York

1,472 feet
102 storie

THE MINUTE I GOT OFF THE PLANE IN NEW YORK, 15,000 PEOPLE STARTED CROWDING AROUND ME. IF YOU DON'T BELIEVE ME, ASK MARLON BRANDO. HE WAS STANDING RIGHT NEXT TO ME!

WILLIAM MORRIS AGENCY, INC.
202 NORTH CANON DRIVE
BEVERLY HILLS, CALIFORNIA

THE AGENCY OF THE SHOW WORLD

AIRMAIL

VIA AIR MA[IL]

Mr. Tommy Cooper
Flamingo Hotel
Las Vegas, Nevada

I STOPPED OFF IN HOLLYWOOD AND MADE TWO PICTURES — FACE FORWARDS AND SIDEWAYS!

Greetings from Las Vegas Nevada

Flamingo

I LOST MY SHIRT IN LAS VEGAS. I MISPLACED MY LAUNDRY TICKET!

FOR THE ACCOUNT OF: Tommy Cooper   No. 26

Payment per contract with Foster Agency, Ltd. dated 3/10/54
Appearance at Flamingo Hotel, Las Vegas W/E 4/21/54
(Piccadilly Revels)

WILLIAM MORRIS AGENCY, INC. COMPENSATION
Advance 4/9 Freeman Transportation Co.
NY baggage transfer   12.30

PLEASE DETACH AND RETAIN THIS VOUCHER BEFORE DEPOSITING
WILLIAM MORRIS AGENCY, INC.
BEVERLY HILLS, CALIF.

WHEN I WAS IN LAS VEGAS I WAS SO UNLUCKY I EVEN LOST MONEY IN THE STAMP MACHINE!

THE Flamingo HOTEL • LAS VEGAS, NEVADA

That's Amore, get solid reaction. Tommy Cooper, zany conjurer, proves highspot of the revue. This veddy British counterpart of our own Ballantine is a magico-satirist whose illusions never come off the way he expects, but the unexpected climaxes to tricks are smooth prestidigitation tailored for laughs. Eddie Vitch gets sidetracked

NEW YORK   BEVERLY HILLS   CHICAGO   LONDON   PARIS
LICENSED ANNUALLY BY L.C.C.
Established 1898
MIFF FERRIE
WILLIAM MORRIS AGENCY INC. NEW YORK
ORCHESTRAS,
(THEATRICAL, ORCHESTRAL & FILM AGE...
25 DURWESTON COURT, WE...

AGVA Standard Form of Artists Engagement Contract

AGREEMENT made this **10th** day of **MARCH**, 195**4**, between
FOSTERS AGENCY LTD. hereinafter called the "Operator" and
TOMMY COOPER hereinafter called the "Artist."

1. The Operator hereby engages the Artist, and the Artist hereby accepts said engagement, to present his act as a **COMEDY MAGICIAN**, consisting of **ONE (1)** persons, at the **FLAMINGO HOTEL** in the City of **LAS VEGAS, NEV.**, for a period of **FIVE 5** consecutive weeks, **SEVEN (7)** days weekly, **FOURTEEN (14)** shows commencing on **APRIL 15th**, 195**4**, for which the Operator agrees to pay the Artist, and the Artist agrees to accept, as full payment, the sum of **TWELVE HUNDRED FIFTY** Dollars ($**1250.00**) weekly, payable immediately preceding the first performance on the concluding night of each week's engagement hereunder.

2. Artist hereby gives and grants to Operator the option of extending this...

PARK CHAMBERS
68 WEST 58th STREET
NEW YORK 19, N. Y.

No. 2327   Apt. No. 408/700   Rate

M Cooper Mr T

DAVY KAYE
"BENNY SOUTHSTREET"
IN
"GUYS & DOLLS"
LONDON COLISEUM
Sole Dir.: WILL COLLINS

THE **PERFORMER**
THE OFFICIAL ORGAN OF THE VARIETY ARTISTES' FEDERATION

THE PREMIER VARIETY JOURNAL

THE
DAGENHAM
GIRL
PIPERS
Entertain the World

VOL. XCVIII. No. 2504   THURSDAY, MAY 20, 1954.   Price 6d.

VARIETY—April 21, 1954

PICCADILLY REVELS FLAMINGO, LAS VEGAS

"... TOMMY COOPER, Zany Conjuror, proves highspot of the Revue"

Sole Direction - - - MIFF FERRIE

	6	7	8	9	10
BROUGHT FORWARD		941	1812	2839	4769
ROOM		7	7	7	7
HOTEL TAX		30	30	30	30
RESTAURANT					
TELEPHONES LOCALS					
TELEPHONES TOLLS					
NEWS.					
VALET					
CASH, C.O.D. ETC.					
TOTAL					
LESS CASH					
TRANSFERS					
ALLOWANCES					
CARRIED FORWARD					

IN LAS VEGAS THEY GAMBLE EVERYWHERE. I WENT INTO A DRUG STORE FOR AN ASPIRIN AND THE GIRL BEHIND THE COUNTER SAID, 'I'LL TOSS YOU, DOUBLE OR NOTHING.' I LOST. I CAME OUT WITH TWO HEADACHES!

IN WITNESS WHEREOF, we have signed this agreement on the day and year first above written.

Artist **TOMMY COOPER**
(Stage Name)
FOSTERS AGENCY LTD.
Operator   By:

12-53-1M

Tommy moved with Dove into the family home in Chiswick towards the end of 1955 and remained there until the end of his days. He never lost touch with family life and wherever he was appearing in the country made an effort to return to relax there every Sunday. By now he and Gwen had two children, Vicky and Thomas.

I LOVE KIDS. I WENT TO SCHOOL WITH THEM!

WHEN MY WIFE WAS PREGNANT WE WENT TO SEE A BABY DOCTOR, BUT HE DIDN'T KNOW ANYTHING. HE WAS ONLY EIGHT MONTHS OLD!

I'VE BEEN LOOKING UP MY FAMILY TREE. THEY WERE ALL ENJOYING THEIR BANANAS!

MY LITTLE BOY SAID TO ME TODAY, 'WHAT DO YOU CALL A GORILLA THAT'S GOT A BANANA IN EACH EAR?' AND I SAID, 'WHAT DO YOU CALL A GORILLA THAT'S GOT A BANANA IN EACH EAR?' HE SAID, 'ANYTHING YOU LIKE – HE CAN'T HEAR YOU!'

'THREE INTO TWO WON'T GO!'

Here is Tommy with two dear friends, Norman Wisdom and Harry Secombe. This rare and distressed image of three kings of comedy was taken on the occasion of the christening of son Thomas. One would like to surmise that had Cooper not died at such a relatively early age, he like the other two would have been dubbed a knight of the realm. When he appeared in the special Royal Gala Performance to celebrate the Queen's Silver Jubilee in 1977, he placed a sword on the stage and kneeled behind it without saying a word. After a few seconds he stood up and returned the weapon to his table shrugging, 'Well, you never know!' The whole theatre – including the royal box – fell about.

HEAD CHOPPER ROUTINE

There isn't any danger, unless of course some-thing goes wrong.
- That I am strictly limited to time, and when the alarm goes off so must I must do likewise.
Ring. Sorry, time's up.

* Just in case it does I'll blindfold you — then you never know what hit you — I MEAN — what happened!!
Perhaps we better not use the blindfold. I'm sure we will proceed while you are still

THIS GUILLOTINE WAS PRESENTED TO ME BY THE MAGIC CIRCLE SO THAT I COULD GET AHEAD!

Tommy made his first series for ITV with *Cooper's Capers* in 1958. This led to many other series for the channel including *Cooperama*, *Life with Cooper* and *The Tommy Cooper Hour*. Here he performs the notorious guillotine trick on actor/presenter Derek Bond on *Cooperama* in 1966. Over the years bandleader Billy Cotton and Michael Parkinson were other notables who found themselves subjected to similar treatment.

6th Augst 1964

My Dear Tommy & Gwen

Thank you for letter I will be coming on Monday 10th inst. I am so glad you will meet me at Waterloo, as I don't like the changing. I get in Waterloo station 12.46pm hope that is alright will you.

I am glad the show is doy so well the reason I thought it was over

was. I see the shows adver in the World Fair, and one week or two it wasn't there, but a couple of days after I wrote to you. I had the W.F. and it was in that week, so then I saw my mistake, so all being well I see you all on Monday.

Love from Mum xx T

I SAID, 'I'M GOING BACK TO MY MOTHER.' MY WIFE SAID, 'THAT'S BETTER THAN HER COMING HERE!'

Tommy became even closer to his mother when his father died in 1963. However, he couldn't write her a straightforward letter without lapsing into joke-speak, as this one found in his files reveals. She continued to run the haberdashery store she opened in the Shirley district of Southampton in 1948 until she was eighty-eight, dying two years later in February 1984, just two months before her famous son.

WHEN THE MIDWIFE TOLD MY MOTHER THAT SHE HAD AN EIGHT POUND BUNDLE OF JOY, MY MOTHER SAID, 'THANK GOD – THE LAUNDRY'S BACK!'

M IS FOR THE MILLION THINGS SHE GAVE ME...
O MEANS THAT SHE'S ONLY GROWING OLD...
T IS FOR THE TEARS SHE SHED TO SAVE ME...
H IS FOR HER HEART SO PURE OF GOLD...
PUT THEM ALTOGETHER...
THEY SPELL MOTH!

Dear Mum,

How nice to hear you are getting on wonderful so well! Looking forward very much seeing you and have a nice long rest with us for you to spend a nice long rest with us. All day yesterday I heard a ringing in my ears — Then I picked up the phone and it stopped. I was going to see my doctor, but he isn't he a very good doctor, all his patients are sick. Dave & myself are on a new diet. We eat our breakfast in the raw. Then we eat our lunch raw. For dinner we put on clothes.

See you soon

All my love

Tommy XXX

DIRECTION : MIFF FERRIE, 29 LOWER BELGRAVIA, LONDON, W.I.   PHONE : SLOANE 0631.

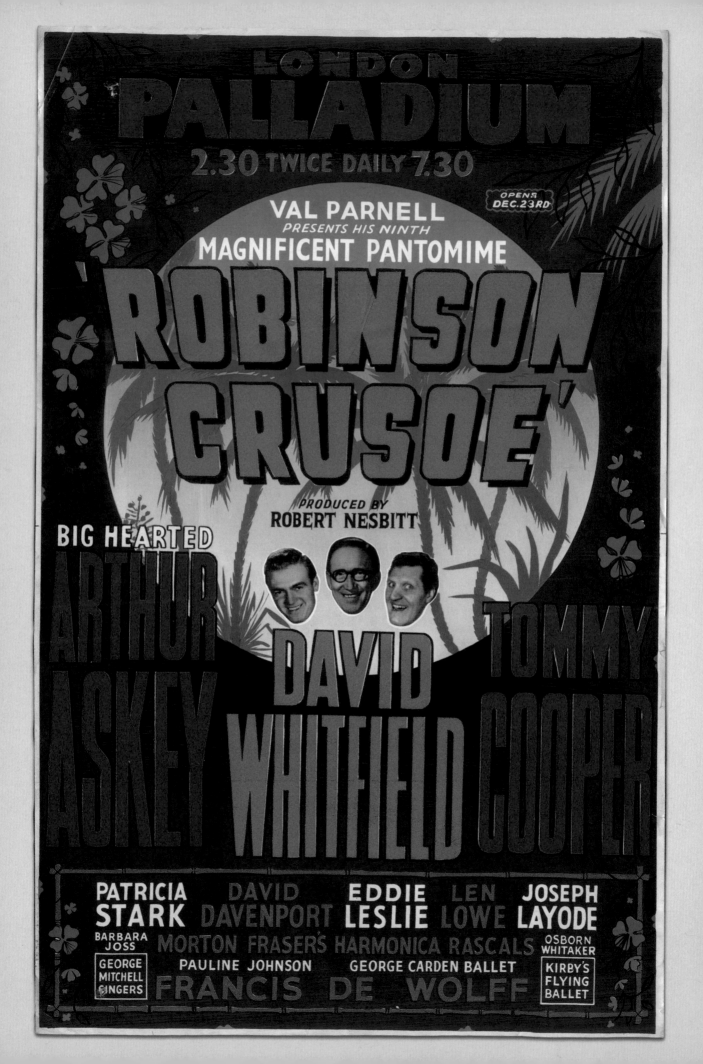

Pantomime became an obvious platform for Tommy's comedy. He first appeared as an unlikely Ugly Sister in *Cinderella* during a tour of northern towns that took in Morecambe, Stockton and Oldham during the 1949/1950 season, but was more at home as 'Abu, a kind of magician', the sidekick to Arthur Askey's Dame, 'Big Hearted Martha', in *Robinson Crusoe* at the London Palladium for Christmas 1957. The run lasted fifteen weeks.

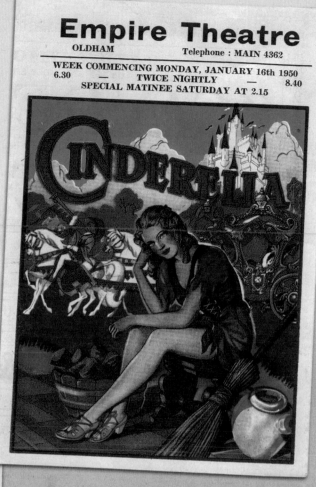

Empire Theatre

OLDHAM   Telephone : MAIN 4362

WEEK COMMENCING MONDAY, JANUARY 16th 1950
6.30 — TWICE NIGHTLY — 8.40
SPECIAL MATINEE SATURDAY AT 2.15

SYD SEYMOUR presents
HIS GREATEST COMEDY AND MOST SPECTACULAR PANTOMIME OF ALL TIMES

"CINDERELLA"
featuring
SYD SEYMOUR
as "BUTTONS"

CONSTANCE EVANS as "CINDERS"	Paddy Dare as "CINDERS"	Jane Austin as "PRINCE CHARMING"	Tania Rusalka as "FAIRY"	COOKE'S PONY REVUE
	GEORGE LAVOIE as "BARON"			

THE SEYMOUR LOVELIES

Wyn McGrath & Luchelle "THE GOOD FAIRIES"	TOMMY COOPER & ANDREWS "UGLY SISTERS" CYRIL		GRAY & KEN "BROKER'S MEN"

AND A SUPER CAST OF SPECIALITIES TO DELIGHT YOUNG AND OLD !

I WAS IN ROBINSON CRUSOE ONCE. I PLAYED HIS MANSERVANT, SHEFFIELD WEDNESDAY!

THE CHRISTMAS PANTOMIME

ROBINSON CRUSOE

At the famous
LONDON PALLADIUM

PROGRAMME PRICE SIXPENCE

HUMPTY DUMPTY SAT ON A WALL,
HUMPTY DUMPTY HAD A GREAT FALL;
ALL THE KING'S HORSES
AND ALL THE KING'S MEN ...
... HAD SCRAMBLED EGGS!

THE NEXT YEAR I PLAYED IN ALADDIN.
I TOUCHED THE LAMP AND THE GENIE
APPEARED. ONE NIGHT I TOUCHED
JEANNIE AND HER HUSBAND APPEARED!

Opening Routine

It's only natural to be nervous at the beginning of a show. — But please don't be.''

He doesn't play bad for a fellow who studied the violin!

The ballet is something I can't understand. All those girls dancing around on their toes. I figure if they want taller girls — why don't they get 'em!!

Instead of a Doctor ~~interwriting~~ prescription were so illegible that a patient used one for 2 years as a Railway Pass, got into theatres and football cup ties with it and finally gave it to his daughter who played it on the Piano and won a scholarship to the ~~Roll~~ Royal Col. of Music!!

I used to be a boxer but I had to give it up. I couldn't learn to pick up my teeth with gloves on!!

I got a kid — listen to this — The other day he had an accident — He went into a barber shop for a haircut and came out with the wrong Head!!

The applause was so deafening, I could hardly hear the Boos!!

Gin, Vodka & Garlic. The garlic tells the waiter which table you're under!!

The manager gave me a nice dressing room but it cost me a penny every time I want to get in!!!

What's the fly doing in my soup. She said, I don't know, he is not one of ours.

I'm on a whiskey diet. ~~Last~~ week I lost 3 days.

I'll be here in person tomorrow night.

Two guys on on the passage talking. One said to the other I hear we might be going out on strike — what are we striking for this time? — He said shorter hours! I'm in favour of that — I always thought sixty minutes was too long!!!

It is no surprise that the most recognisable man in British show business quickly became a target for caricaturists and cartoonists throughout the land. He was first featured in the pages of the children's comic *Film Fun* in the mid-fifties, joining the famous company of Abbott and Costello, Frankie Howerd and two of his heroes, Laurel and Hardy. By the end of the decade he had taken over pole position on the front page.

WHAT A RECEPTION I GOT WHEN I STEPPED OFF THE PLANE. EVERYBODY STARTED SHOUTING, 'THERE'S TONY CURTIS! THERE'S TONY CURTIS!' SO I TURNED AROUND AND THERE WAS TONY CURTIS!

A CHAP CAME OVER TO ME IN THE PUB THE OTHER DAY AND SAID, 'I SAW YOU IN *CORONATION STREET* LAST WEEK ... GREAT!' 'SORRY,' I SAID, 'I WASN'T IN *CORONATION STREET*.' 'I'M SURE I SAW YOU IN *CORONATION STREET*,' HE INSISTED. I STILL SHOOK MY HEAD. THEN HE THOUGHT HARD FOR A WHILE, GRIPPED MY ARM AND SAID, 'NO, THAT'S RIGHT – I SAW YOU IN SAINSBURY'S!'

No mistaking the man on the magazine covers. It was just unlucky for Tommy that two of his most prestigious front pages were reduced to black and white when they coincided with industrial action in the printing trade and had to be brought out in slimline emergency editions.

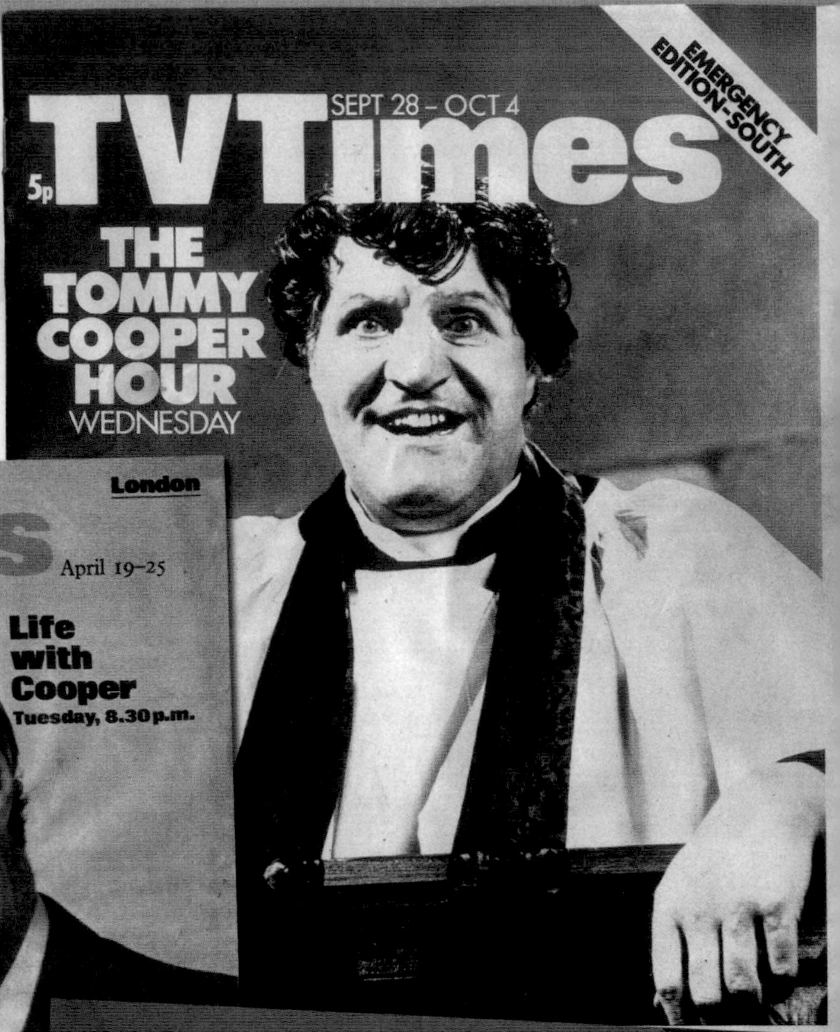

EMERGENCY EDITION-SOUTH

TVTimes
SEPT 28 – OCT 4
5p
THE TOMMY COOPER HOUR
WEDNESDAY

TVTimes
London
Sixpence
April 19-25
Emergency Edition
– See back page
Life with Cooper
Tuesday, 8.30p.m.

TVTimes
6p
APRIL 20-26
TOMMY COOPER
MY PANIC BEFORE THE SHOW
SEE PAGE 34
Join the £10,000 search for
THE PUB ENTERTAINER OF THE YEAR
SEE PAGE 20

DO YOU KNOW NOELE GORDON'S DOUBLE? If you do, you can be a star student at Crossroads party
HOW VALERIE SAINT BECAME COOK OF COOKS The meal that tempted the stars and won a £5,000 kitchen

TVTimes
13p
JULY 1-7
Three tricks you can do like Tommy Cooper...
JUST LIKE THAT
See page 16

WEEKEND
13p No. 3834 AUGUST 23-29, 1978

BEDTIME SECRETS OF THE SIAMESE TWINS PAGE 12

Tommy Cooper tells of...

THE NIGHT I NEARLY DIED

PATRICK'S DEBUT IN A FIG LEAF
Cushiest jail on earth PAGES 18, 19

ATTACKED BY RUSSIAN JETS

WAISTCOAT WITH PATTERNED FRONT TO KNIT

TRUE-LIFE DRAMA

...cared to Tommy Cooper. He even jokes about...

NIGHT I NEARLY DIED
By DICK MAINO

Minutes before he was due to go on stage, he collapsed. Now his whole life has changed

Cigars are banned from Tommy's act now

FUNNYMAN

Name: Tommy Cooper. Occupation: laughter-maker. Trademarks: crazy cackle, tricks that don't work, and a fez. Credentials: twelve million viewers for his TV shows, which usually nudge the top of the ratings. Income: up to £4,000 a week / by Kenneth Eastaugh

HIS TRICKS NEVER WORK— BUT HE'S MAGIC

Tommy Cooper is the world's worst conjurer, but when he gets up on stage everyone starts applauding, just like that. After he'd left the audience rolling in the aisles, John Sandilands went home with him to find out what really goes on under that red fez

He's a lovely man really— his children think the world of him. Mind you, they think he's a bit eccentric— but he is, isn't he?

Tommy, in a favourite funny hat, takes off on the piano

The JOKER
VOL 2 NO3 15p
Britain's Top laughter magazine

SPRING ISSUE

spring sunshine with Giant Joker of the Month Tommy Cooper

PLUS - exclusive - CHARLIE SMITHERS COMEDIAN OF THE YEAR
PLUS - BOB MONKHOUSE IN DARKEST AFRICA
PLUS - ROY CASTLE - HAPPY IN HIS HOME

CURED— JUST LIKE THAT!
BY MARY BOWEN

Doctors feared Tommy Cooper had been struck down by a heart attack—but now he can see the funny side

"...he's a star"

When Tommy Cooper goes on stage, it's aggravated assault on the funny bone. But away from the limelight, it's not like that! He's a driven man: an insomniac, a perfectionist and, his wife says, a hypochondriac. In this, one of an occasional series on Britain's funniest men, Chris Greenwood talks to the comic who just doesn't understand he's one of the biggest, brightest belly-tickling stars in show-biz....

GIANT-SIZE comic Tommy Cooper has such an irrepressible sense of humour he can even turn his troubles into a laugh.

These images were taken for a magazine profile that appears never to have been published; it certainly did not survive in the files of either Tommy or his agent. They perfectly convey the side of Cooper that refused ever to grow up, a key factor in why his comedy remains ageless and seemingly effortless today. It is not difficult to tell from these pictures who is enjoying himself more – father or son.

WHAT A WONDERFUL DAY IT'S BEEN. SEVENTY DEGREES IN THE SHADE. I WAS CLEVER – I STAYED IN THE SUN!

THE TROUBLE WITH KIDS TODAY IS THEY GET SPOILED TOO FAST. I SPENT TWENTY POUNDS ON A SPACE SUIT FOR MY LITTLE BOY AND THEN HE WOULDN'T GO!

WATCH OUT FOR CHILDREN ON THE ROADS ... THEY'RE TERRIBLE DRIVERS!

I CAME HOME FROM SCHOOL ONE DAY AND TOLD MY FATHER I NEEDED AN ENCYCLOPAEDIA. HE SAID, 'ENCYCLOPAEDIA, MY EYE! YOU'LL WALK TO SCHOOL LIKE EVERYONE ELSE!'

ONE BIRTHDAY MY FATHER BOUGHT ME A BAT. WHEN I WENT TO PLAY WITH IT, IT FLEW AWAY!

Tommy fell in love with magic as a boy and spent all his pocket money on tricks and jokes which he saw advertised in children's comics. In later life he was seldom happier than when pursuing in private the more serious side of the craft that he guyed so relentlessly on stage. He was a welcome visitor at all the top magic depots in London, whose catalogues provide more than a few reminders of his act. When he was asked to reopen the famous Ellisdons store in High Holborn, he was in seventh heaven.

WHEN I'M NOT DOING TRICKS, I PUT ON A FLOOR SHOW – I DEMONSTRATE VACUUM CLEANERS!

THE MAGIC CIRCULAR.

Vol. 43.   SEPTEMBER 1949.   No. 481.

THE ANNUAL
Grand FESTIVAL OF MAGIC
SCALA THEATRE, W.C.I., OCTOBER 3rd, 1949,
SIX NIGHTS at 7-15 p.m.
MATINEES WEDNESDAY & SATURDAY, 2-30.
(This Theatre is less than one minute from Goodge Street Tube Station.)

An Outstanding All-Star Programme :

CLAUDE CHANDLER.   TOMMY COOPER.
D'ALBERT.   DOMINIQUE.
DOUGLAS FRANCIS.   GEORGE GRIMMOND.
JACK LEDAIR.

DAVID NIXON—Compere.   JOHN YOUNG—Prologue.

BOOK NOW AND AVOID DISAPPOINTMENT.

Box "B" (six seats) 16/- per seat.
Stalls 15/- 12·6 10·6 7·6   Dress Circle 15/- 12·6 10·6
Circle 7·6 6·9   Upper Circle 5/- 3·6

Send remittance and stamped addressed envelope to :—
Mr. E. G. BRITTIAN, 57, Chatsworth Way, West Norwood, S.E.27.
State clearly which performance. Be wise—book early.
The 15/- Seats for the Friday and Saturday are all sold. Plenty left at 12·6
downwards.

NOTE.— On and after September 5th, the Booking must
be done direct with the Scala Theatre.   Mus 5731.

MAKE ONE BIG FINAL EFFORT PLEASE TO GET
YOUR FRIENDS & THE PUBLIC INTERESTED.

Tommy was never more proud than when he was elevated
to membership of The Inner Magic Circle by the President,
Francis White, in 1966.

JUNE, 1957

THE MAGIC CIRCULAR

I'M A MEMBER OF THE MAGIC CIRCLE. I AM ALSO
A MEMBER OF THE SECRET SIX. IT'S SO SECRET
I DON'T EVEN KNOW THE OTHER FIVE!

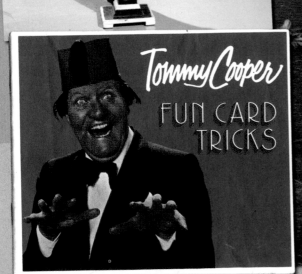

Tommy Cooper
FUN CARD TRICKS

NOW I WANT YOU TO TAKE A CARD — ANY CARD. NOW TEAR
IT INTO HALVES — TEAR IT INTO QUARTERS — TEAR IT INTO
EIGHTHS — AND THROW THE PIECES UP IN THE AIR. INSTANT
CONFETTI! HAPPY NEW YEAR!

THE HAND IS QUICKER THAN THE EYE –
THAT'S WHY YOU SEE SO MANY BLACK EYES!

JAR, SPOON!
SPOON, JAR!

HERE'S THE BOTTLE AND
HERE'S THE GLASS. THE
BOTTLE WILL NOW CHANGE
PLACES WITH THE GLASS!

MAGIC! WHAT I DON'T
KNOW ABOUT MAGIC
WOULD FILL AN
AIRCRAFT HANGAR!

TEACH
YOURSELF
MAGIC

NOW THIS DUCK WILL TAKE YOUR CHOSEN
CARD FROM THAT PACK. NOW YOU MAY HAVE
SEEN A DUCK DO THAT BEFORE – BUT TO BE
FAIR, BLINDFOLDED?

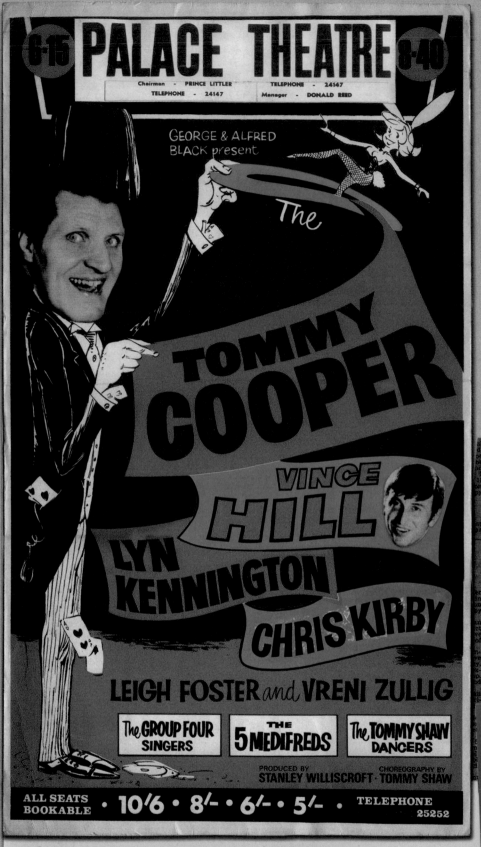

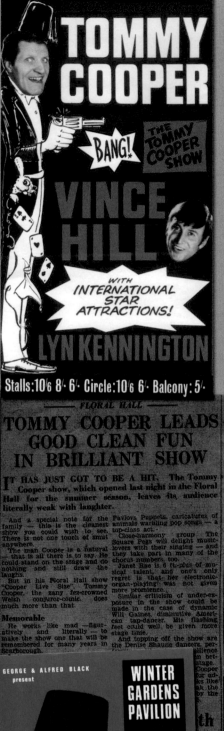

The summer months often saw Tommy starring in spectacular summer shows at the nation's top resorts including Bournemouth, Blackpool, Scarborough, Skegness, Torquay and Margate. He immortalised the latter in one of his funniest patter routines. The shot of Tommy and Gwen strolling along the seafront at Eastbourne was taken in 1948.

FIRST I DO THE BREASTSTROKE FOR TWO HOURS AND THEN I DO THE CRAWL FOR THREE HOURS. THEN I GO IN THE WATER AND WASH THE SAND OFF!

MY WIFE AND I USED TO HAVE SUCH FUN AT THE BEACH. FIRST SHE WOULD BURY ME IN THE SAND, THEN I WOULD BURY HER IN THE SAND. ONE OF THESE DAYS I'M GOING TO GO BACK AND DIG HER UP!

FLORAL HALL
Scarborough Telephone 2185

General Manager: A.D. EASTON F.I.M. Ent. Licensee & Manager: A. HATTERSLEY

COMMENCING TUESDAY, 17th. JUNE, 1969 at 8 p.m. and THEREAFTER

TWICE NIGHTLY (except sundays) 6·15 and 8·40 until sept.13th.

RICHARD STONE presents

TOMMY COOPER

IN

COOPER LIVE-SIZE

A **FREDDIE CARPENTER** PRODUCTION

Choreography by DENISE SHAUNE WITH

JOAN SAVAGE

DENISE SHAUNE DANCERS WITH

WILL GAINES

* ROY CAVAL *

PAVLOV'S PUPPETS * **JANET RAE**

TOMMY WATT and HIS MUSIC

THE SQUARE PEGS

10/- centre stalls * 8/6 rear stalls * 7/6 side stalls * 5/- side boxes
children half price 6·15 performances Friday & Saturday only

FLORAL HALL
SCARBOROUGH
PROGRAMME ONE SHILLING

RICHARD STONE PRESENTS

TOMMY COOPER IN **COOPER LIVE SIZE**

R: A. D. EASTON, F.I.M.Ent. LICENSEE & MANAGER: A. HATTERSLEY

Bernard Delfont presents

Show Time

DEVISED & PRODUCED BY ERNEST MAXIN

at the **PRINCESS THEATRE** TORQUAY

PROGRAMME ONE SHILLING

PRINCESS THEATRE
TORQUAY Telephone 7527

Commencing Wednesday, June 7th

NIGHTLY at 6 and 8.30 Throughout the Season

BERNARD DELFONT presents

* **JOAN REGAN** *

TOMMY COOPER * **EDMUND HOCKRIDGE**

MORECAMBE & WISE

plus FULL COMPANY in

"SHOW TIME"

Devised and Produced by ERNEST MAXIN

BOX OFFICE OPEN DAILY
10 a.m. — 8 p.m.

STALLS 8/6, 6/-
CIRCLE 8/6, 6/-, 5/-

SOMEBODY RANG MY WIFE AND SAID,
'I SAW YOUR HUSBAND ON THE BEACH
WITH A BLONDE ON HIS ARM.' SHE
SAID, 'WHAT DO YOU EXPECT AT HIS
AGE — A BUCKET AND SPADE?'

NORTH PIER
Pavilion
BLACKPOOL
TEL. 20980

OPENING FRIDAY JUNE 7TH | TWICE NIGHTLY 6·0 & 8·30 | MATINEE WEDNESDAY 2·30

BERNARD DELFONT PRESENTS

3 GREAT STARS

PLUS A **TERRIFIC CAST**

RUBY MURRAY **TOMMY COOPER**

KEN PLATT

A LONDON WEST-END PRODUCTION BRIMFUL OF COMEDY! DEVISED & PRODUCED BY ERNEST MAXIN

IN HIS FIRST COLOSSAL SUMMER SHOW

Show Time

TOMMY COOPER

QUEEN'S THEATRE, BLACKPOOL - SUMMER SEASON

WEST LANCASHIRE EVENING GAZETTE. 7th June, 1965.

".....TOMMY COOPER of course has only to turn up on stage to raise the roof, and in this show he is funnier than ever....."

BOLTON EVENING NEWS, 7th June, 1965.

".....TOMMY COOPER, too, has his solo spots larking madly and irrepressibly in both parts of the show, and bringing the laughs with his lunatic antics......"

MUSICAL EXPRESS, 11th June, 1965.

".....and TOMMY COOPER funnier than ever........"

DAILY MAIL, 7th June, 1965.

".....The good things?   At the Queen's Theatre TOMMY COOPER - Very very funny, throwing away jokes as reckless as ever....."

"BLACKPOOL NIGHT OUT" - TELEVISION.

EVENING TELEGRAPH AND POST, 21st June, 1965.

".....and of course there was fumbling and fantastically funny TOMMY COOPER......."

TELEVISION TODAY, 24th June, 1965.

"ONLY TOMMY BIG ENOUGH TO SURVIVE - His irrepressible good humour and effervescent personality making him seem even bigger physically than he actually is....."

DERBY EVENING TELEGRAPH, 21st June, 1965.

"BLACKPOOL NIGHT OUT, ITV's summer successor to the Palladium Show last night, was a refreshing change from the stereotype formula that has been with us for so many months...... Top of the bill was the incomparable TOMMY COOPER who never fails to rock the joint with laughter...."

SUNDAY MAIL, GLASGOW, 27th June, 1965.

"It's a long time since I've laughed so much,
        I laughed till I was sore,
At Tommy Cooper's antics,
        Wish we could see him more,
His tricks are good, he's full of fun,
        Well worth our licence fee,
I wish that he was staying,
        In the house next door to me."

SUNDAY MIRROR, 27th June, 1965.

".....I could have watched TOMMY COOPER all night....."

EVENING STAR, IPSWICH, 21st June, 1965.

".....It was TOMMY COOPER as usual who gave the whole show a touch of greatness.   This surely is one of the funniest men around today....."

DAILY MIRROR, 21st June, 1965.

".....TOMMY COOPER as always had me convulsed....."

EVENING CITIZEN, GLASGOW, 19th June, 1965.

".....One especially good thing about tomorrow's Opening, TOMMY COOPER is there also....."

A FRIEND OF MINE SAID YOU WANT TO GO TO MARGATE – IT'S GOOD FOR RHEUMATISM. SO I WENT AND I GOT IT!

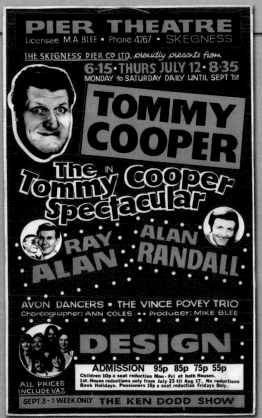

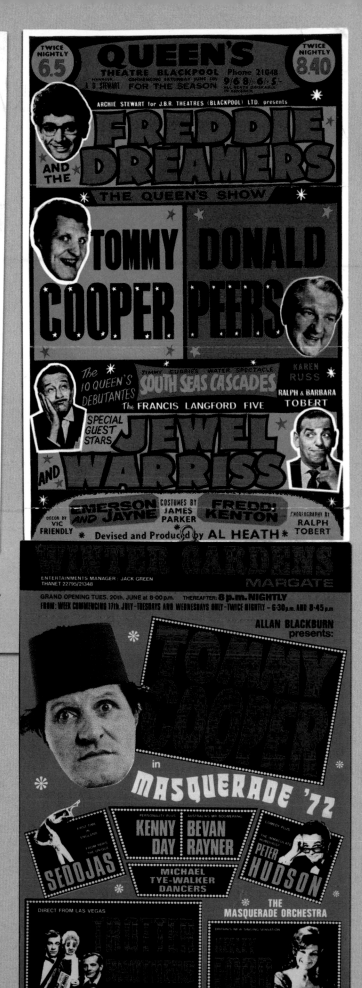

Always keen to help servicemen's charities, Tommy and Dove returned to the Middle East to give moral support in later years. A visit to a street market in Cairo gave birth to one of his favourite anecdotes.

WHEN WE WENT BACK TO EGYPT, THERE WAS THIS GUY SELLING FEZZES IN THE MARKET. I WENT TO TRY ONE ON AND HE TURNED TO ME AND SAID, 'JUS' LIKE THAT!' I SAID, 'HOW DO YOU KNOW THAT? THAT'S MY CATCHPHRASE.' HE SAID, 'CATCHPHRASE? I KNOW NOTHING ABOUT ANY CATCHPHRASE. ALL I KNOW IS THAT EVERY TIME AN ENGLISH PERSON TRIES ONE ON, THEY TURN TO THEIR FRIENDS AND SAY, "JUS' LIKE THAT!"' AND THEN HE SAID, 'YOU'RE THE FIRST ONE NOT TO SAY IT.' PRICELESS, ISN'T IT?

He first wore the fez in Cairo during a wartime show for the YMCA when he mislaid the pith helmet he was wearing in his act at the time and grabbed the fez off a passing waiter to make amends.

MY WIFE ALWAYS SERVES ME FOOD THAT MELTS IN THE MOUTH, BUT HOW MANY ICE CUBES CAN A MAN SWALLOW?

Tommy's favourite food included Dove's special raspberry sponge, marked out by its triple layers to maximise the jam content!

I SAID TO MY WIFE, 'I CAN'T EAT THIS BEEF STEW.' SHE SAID, 'SHUT UP! IT'S CUSTARD PIE!'

The comments in red pencil are Tommy's own!

SHE SAID, 'THE STOVE HAS GONE OUT.' I SAID, 'LIGHT IT.' SHE SAID, 'I CAN'T. IT'S GONE OUT THROUGH THE CEILING!'

SHE'S SUCH A TERRIBLE COOK, FOR TEN YEARS SHE THOUGHT POACHED EGGS WERE ILLEGAL!

SHE COOKS SO BAD, THE CAT HAS ONLY THREE LIVES LEFT!

Tommy used to boast that he had the best wife in England – the other one was in Africa! She was the strictest judge of his material and would time his rehearsals at home with a stopwatch, leaving spaces for the laughs. 'She knows exactly how long they'll be. She says, "Do this, do that, move that trick somewhere else and then finish your act with such-and-such." She's always right. She's never wrong.' In return the family home became a minefield of practical jokes as trick spiders turned up in the bath and plastic beetles on the breakfast tray. Kitchen items – not least the clock on the wall – would go missing and not be seen again until they cropped up in his act. No aspect of domestic routine was sacred.

I CAN'T STAND MY WIFE SMOKING IN BED. I KNOW A LOT OF WOMEN SMOKE IN BED, BUT FACE DOWN?

MY WIFE JUST PHONED ME BEFORE THE SHOW. SHE SAID, 'I'VE GOT WATER IN THE CARBURETTOR.' I SAID, 'WHERE'S THE CAR?' SHE SAID, 'IN THE RIVER!'

MY WIFE CAME IN THE OTHER DAY AND SHE SAID, 'WHAT'S DIFFERENT ABOUT ME?' AND I SAID, 'I DON'T KNOW – WHAT IS DIFFERENT ABOUT YOU? HAVE YOU HAD YOUR HAIR DONE?' SHE SAID, 'NO.' I SAID, 'HAVE YOU GOT A NEW DRESS ON?' SHE SAID, 'NO.' I SAID, 'HAVE YOU GOT A NEW PAIR OF SHOES?' SHE SAID, 'NO.' I SAID, 'WELL WHAT IS IT? WHAT'S DIFFERENT ABOUT YOU?' SHE SAID, 'I'M WEARING A GAS MASK!'

The methods in the madness of the dysfunctional magician were never more apparent than in the Polaroids taken as an exact record of what went where in his act. As one stagehand observed, the minutes before he went on stage were like a space launch countdown.

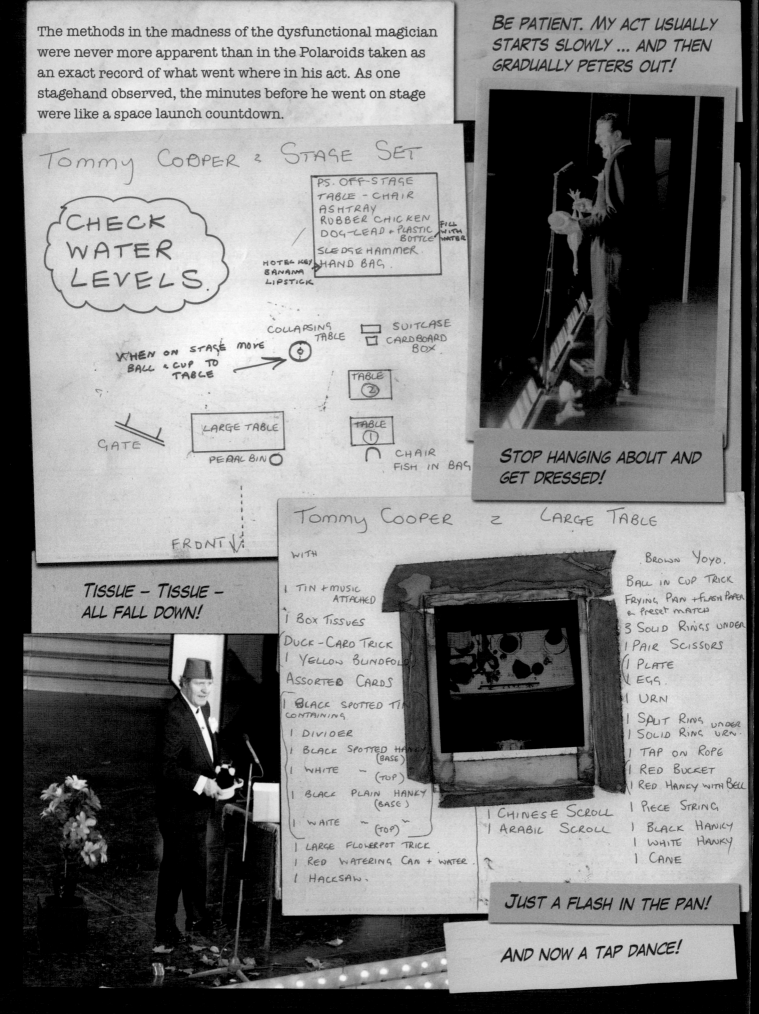

BE PATIENT. MY ACT USUALLY STARTS SLOWLY ... AND THEN GRADUALLY PETERS OUT!

STOP HANGING ABOUT AND GET DRESSED!

Tommy Cooper 2 Stage Set

CHECK WATER LEVELS.

P.S. OFF-STAGE
TABLE - CHAIR
ASHTRAY
RUBBER CHICKEN
DOG-LEAD + PLASTIC BOTTLE
SLEDGE HAMMER.
HAND BAG.

FILL WITH WATER

HOTEL KEY
BANANA
LIPSTICK

WHEN ON STAGE MOVE BALL + CUP TO TABLE

COLLAPSING TABLE

SUITCASE
CARDBOARD BOX.

GATE

LARGE TABLE
PEDAL BIN

TABLE 2
TABLE 1
CHAIR
FISH IN BAG

FRONT ↓

TISSUE - TISSUE - ALL FALL DOWN!

Tommy Cooper 2 Large Table

WITH

1 TIN + MUSIC ATTACHED
1 BOX TISSUES
DUCK-CARD TRICK
1 YELLOW BLINDFOLD
ASSORTED CARDS
1 BLACK SPOTTED TIN CONTAINING
1 DIVIDER
1 BLACK SPOTTED HANKY (BASE)
1 WHITE ~ (TOP)
1 BLACK PLAIN HANKY (BASE)
1 WHITE ~ (TOP)
1 LARGE FLOWERPOT TRICK
1 RED WATERING CAN + WATER.
1 HACKSAW.

1 CHINESE SCROLL
1 ARABIC SCROLL

BROWN YOYO.
BALL IN CUP TRICK
FRYING PAN + FLASH PAPER & PRESET MATCH
3 SOLID RINGS UNDER
1 PAIR SCISSORS
1 PLATE
1 EGG.
1 URN
1 SPLIT RING UNDER
1 SOLID RING URN.
1 TAP ON ROPE
1 RED BUCKET
1 RED HANKY WITH BELL
1 PIECE STRING
1 BLACK HANKY
1 WHITE HANKY
1 CANE

JUST A FLASH IN THE PAN!

AND NOW A TAP DANCE!

Tommy Cooper's Table ①

WITH

~~—~~

LARGE METAL
BUCKET
ROUND / SQUARE
TRICK

1 SPLIT RING
1 SOLID RING
TOP HAT

4 SHORT CONNECTED
STRINGS.

2 TUBES
1 WITH large & Small
Bottles & Glass
1 with Glass

FRONT

Tommy Cooper 2 Table ②

WITH —

1 SWORD.
1 BOUQUET
1 Sowester
1 Skipping Rope
NEWSPAPER UNDER —
1 BODY BUILDER
1 TIN OF Bounce
1 RED CYLINDER
1 GREEN CYLINDER
(INSIDE RED)
GOLDFISH BOWL
FLOWERPOT & FLOWER
(RED)
1 PLASTIC ARMY HAT

FRONT

HERE WE HAVE A SKIPPING ROPE —
SO WE'LL SKIP THAT!

Tommy Cooper's Small Box

CONTAINING

BLACK DICE
CLIP ON HAND
MOP CAP
CLIP ON HOLLY
JOINT OF MEAT

Tommy Cooper's Blue Suitcase

CONTAINING

3 INDIAN CLUBS
1 POP-UP-STOOL
1 HAT RING
3 BOWLS (1 FALSE)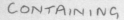
1 BALL IN CUP TRICK
1 BLACK PLASTIC BALL

AFTER THE SHOW YOU ALL HAVE TO WRITE TWENTY-FIVE WORDS ON 'WHY I LIKE TOMMY COOPER.' ALL ENTRIES MUST BE WRITTEN ON A TWENTY POUND NOTE!

NOW TO FINISH I'D JUST LIKE TO SING YOU ONE LITTLE SONG – 'WHEN YOU WALK THROUGH THE STORM, WITH YOUR HEAD HELD HIGH' – I DID AND I FELL IN A RIVER!

WHAT AN AUDIENCE! I HAD THEM EATING OUT OF MY HAND. THEY MUST HAVE THOUGHT THEY WERE AT THE ZOO!

8th May 1964

Tommy Cooper Esq.,
51 Barrowgate Road,
LONDON, W.4.

Dear Tommy,

LONDON PALLADIUM SHOW

I am writing you in reference to the playing time
that has been allocated to you in connection with your prop-
osed two main appearances in the forthcoming Palladium Show.

Robert Nesbitt tells me that under no circumstances
must each appearance exceed that of 12-minutes.

Please, Tommy, at all times, have this matter well
in your mind and arrange your material accordingly.

May I take this opportunity of wishing you every
success in this show.

Kind regards,

Yours sincerely,
For BERNARD DELFONT LIMITED

BILLY MARSH
DIRECTOR

Like all the top performers of his generation
Tommy had a soft spot for the London Palladium.
He first appeared there in a bill headed by the
now forgotten American comedy team Peter
Lind Hayes & Mary Healy in July 1952. He
returned many times over the years, notably
for the special Coronation variety season with
US comic Danny Thomas in 1953 and co-starring
with Frankie Vaughan and Cilla Black in *Startime!*
in 1964.

ONE WEEK I HAD TO SHARE MY
DRESSING ROOM WITH A MONKEY.
THE PRODUCER CAME IN AND SAID,
'I'M SORRY ABOUT THIS.' I SAID,
'THAT'S OKAY.' HE SAID, 'I WASN'T
TALKING TO YOU!'

PALLADIUM

LESLIE A. MACDONNELL &
BERNARD DELFONT present
Startime!

THE FAMOUS
LONDON
PALLADIUM

BOOK NOW!

THE PRESS ACCLAIM ANOTHER
ALL-STAR PALLADIUM HIT!

LESLIE A. MACDONNELL & BERNARD DELFONT
present

FRANKIE
VAUGHAN
with
THE 'V' GROUP
in
Startime!

With
TOMMY COOPER
CILLA BLACK
THE FOURMOST
PETER GOODWRIGHT
AUDREY JEANS
FRANCIS BRUNN

THE PALLADIUM BOYS & GIRLS
THE PALLADIUM ORCHESTRA DIRECTED BY BILLY TERNENT

"FRANKIE VAUGHAN, CILLA BLACK, TOMMY COOPER, PETER
GOODWRIGHT AND THE FOURMOST, MAKE UP AN EXCELLENT
BILL AT THE LONDON PALLADIUM. *TAKE THE FAMILY
TO THIS SPARKLING SHOW.*"
— News of the World

★ FRANKIE VAUGHAN
...splendid, inexhaustible Frankie Vaughan.
— The Guardian
Frankie Vaughan showed what it takes to
stay a bill-topper....
— Daily Mirror
Mr. Vaughan alone is worth the price of the
ticket. A voice that can capture an
audience.
— Daily Sketch
No artiste ever spread out his hands with
more determination to please and it is only
fair to say that he has a large part of the
audience eating out of both of them.
— Daily Mail
Frankie Vaughan looking younger than ever,
tops the bill and still makes the girls
squeal with delight.
— Evening News
Mr. Vaughan is a top-class professional
showman.
— The Times

★ TOMMY COOPER
...Tommy Cooper's marvellous and zany
performance...
— Daily Sketch
Tommy is tops...Bless him, he is a very
funny man...for me, the best sound of
the night, was the noise of the laughter
generated by Tommy Cooper.
— Daily Herald
Tommy Cooper won big laughs.
— Daily Mirror

★ CILLA BLACK
— Evening News
Cilla wins me over.
Cilla hits the West End...without doubt the
biggest star potential since Shirley Bassey.
— Daily Express
Oh! to be in London now that Cilla's here!
— The Guardian

THE FOURMOST
...for sheer charm
they stole the show.
— The Times

PETER GOODWRIGHT
Peter Goodwright is
just honestly funny...
— The Guardian

★ AUDREY JEANS
Audrey Jeans was at her best with
impressions of an old-time star singing
current hit parade numbers.
— Daily Mirror
Audrey Jeans is the splendid trouper who,
above everybody else is making the Palladium
the real music hall of the sixties.
— The Guardian
Audrey Jeans, here is a natural for a Musical
Show. She has a great sense of fun, she can
dance and she can sing, and she has a
pleasing personality.
— Evening News

FRANCIS BRUNN
...described as a "juggling sensation"
but this is an under-statement.
— D. Telegraph
Juggling can bore, but not Francis Brunn.
— The Guardian

He eventually appeared as undisputed top of the bill in the revue *To See Such Fun!* in 1971.

I'LL NEVER FORGET WHEN I WAS PLAYING THE PALLADIUM ... I DREW A LINE A MILE LONG, BUT THE MANAGER MADE ME GO OUT AND ERASE IT!

sincerity, plugging their latest hits.

Tommy Cooper heads the current bill and, even if he takes time to warm up, he still has the manic quality of the true comic eccentric. All the old trademarks are there: the gratuitous fez, the shoulder-heaving delight at his own excruciating oneliners, the conjuring tricks that disastrously misfire. Indeed to see Mr. Cooper toss an egg into the air and then look on with blank astonishment as it shatters the plate on which it was supposed to land is to get an inkling of what music hall humour really is.

Feast of fun

THE CRAZY antics and cockeyed party tricks of **Tommy Cooper** made me nearly split my sides laughing.

His repertoire ranged from turning a handkerchief into a rubber pigeon to pouring the same quantity of milk from one glass to another in glasses of four different sizes.

In the glittering £80,000 summer spectacular at the Palladium, he was strongly supported by a tip-top line up including Russ Conway, better than ever and giving a memorable rendering of 'The Theme from Love Story' and 'Exodus', Clive Dunn bumbling to great effect, and Anita Harris putting her heart and soul into the two songs 'Just Loving You' and 'The Impossible Dream'.

A real feast of fun for the whole family.

Between 1963 and 1967 Tommy recorded a total of five appearances for America's celebrated *The Ed Sullivan Show*. On one occasion Sullivan referred to him as 'the funniest man ever to appear on this stage.' That the host allowed himself to be made the fall guy in one of Cooper's tricks is a measure of his regard for him.

April 11th, 1963

Mr. Miff Ferrie
50 Eaton Terrace
London, S.W.1, England

My dear Ferrie:

Received your letter of the 5th and I do appreciate your co-operation.

Happy to report that TOMMY COOPER'S reaction was fine and at some future date that will be agreeable all around, I have the feeling that they would like him back on the Sullivan Show.   You do not have to answer on this right away but I am curious as to what Tommy's two other spots consist of.

Received quite a few calls but none of a startling nature.   I am concentrating on Lake Tahoe, Reno, Vegas, Miami Beach, the Latin Quarter and Radio City Music Hall, etcetra but I am notifying everyone that Tommy is not available for a long time.   What I am doing is trying to sow some seeds for the future and I am also after a long term spot in a TV series, not forgetting the motion picture companies.

Think the enclosed contract speaks for itself.   This is for the taped show tommy did the afternoon of March 31st for the sum of $1500.   Please have all contracts signed and initial the clause "Q" which calls for a fifty percent fee for replay but take into consideration that the hat bit was done live and on tape but if there is any replays, you will be collecting on this also.   Please return all three copies of the contract as soon as they have been properly signed and initialled.   Just as soon as the payment is issued for the taped show, I will forward you my check for same, less the five percent commission.

Enclosed is check No.25723 from the Ed Sullivan Office, in the sum of $972.00, made payable to Tommy Cooper and representing the transportation advanced for the two round trip fares to New York.

Am also enclosing my check for $4275.00 which represents payment for the March 24th and 31st live shows and trust this meets with your approval.

Again, happy as hell with the results we got from Tommy Cooper.

All good wishes.

Sincerely,

M. J. Leddy

MJL:LW   MARK J. LEDDY

Apart from his successes in America, Tommy made several less likely visits to perform in foreign climes. His British television shows were popular in Scandinavia and the Benelux countries and led to personal appearances on Dutch TV. In the spring of 1967 he performed in cabaret at Hong Kong's famous Mandarin Hotel. This was not his most auspicious season. In spite of glowing local reviews, the Chinese, conditioned by their save face culture, could not bring themselves to laugh at the supposed failure of his magic tricks!

TOMMY KEEPS ALL IN STITCHES

A memory coloured by the distance of childhood is the hilarity of the circus clown. Tommy Cooper this month in the Mandarin Button Club recalls that memory with more laughter than a clown could ever have made on his own.

In the semi-darkness before the show, the cluttered tables and props of a magician are carried out and set up. Mr. Cooper follows in a blaze of light looking like a grizzly bear wearing a fez.

The STAR, Hongkong, Wednesday, April 12, 1967, Page 13.

He's very, very funn

TOMMY Cooper is funnier than Tony Hancock!

Well, that's our opinion anyway, after seeing Cooper at the Mandarin Button Supper Club. You couldn't get two other comedians whose styles are as different as those of Hancock and Cooper.

Hancock has that giant...

...joying them.

And at the end, bow-tied members of the audience whistled for more.

He's the first entertainer at the Mandarin we've seen to get such a good reception.

STAR ENTERTAINM

DESCRIPTION² SIGNALEMENT

	Bearer Titulaire	★Wife Femme
Profession / Profession	ARTIST.	
Place and date of birth / Lieu et date de naissance	CAERPHILLY WALES MAR. 19TH 1921	
Country of Residence / Pays de Résidence	ENGLAND	
Height / Taille	6 ft. 3 in.	ft. in.
Colour of eyes / Couleur des yeux	BLUE	
Colour of hair / Couleur des cheveux	BROWN.	
Special peculiarities / Signes particuliers		

★CHILDREN ENFANTS

Name Nom | Date of birth Date de naissance | Sex Sexe

Usual signature of bearer
Signature du titulaire

Usual signature of wife
Signature de sa femme

Bearer
Titulaire

Wife
Femme

MR. T. F. COOPER.

BRITISH PASSPORT

UNITED KINGDOM OF GREAT BRITAIN AND NORTHERN IRELAND

164483

THE ONLY TIME MOST PEOPLE LOOK LIKE THEIR PASSPORT PHOTOS IS DURING A HIJACK!

Hong Kong

Juggling Props & Vase, Flowers. Flower Pot Stand. Duck Pan, & Comedy Duck.

What's On
in HONGKONG

Free of Charge
April 1967

see Night Life Section

The photo shows Tommy and Gwen at the Mandarin Hotel on 3rd April 1967.

DID YOU EVER TRY TO EAT WITH CHOPSTICKS? I TRIED IT ONCE. I DIDN'T EAT ANYTHING, BUT I STARTED THREE FIRES!

The **Mandarin**
HONG KONG

16th April, 1967.

Miss Kai Yin Lo,
Public Relations,
Mandarin Hotel.

WHEN I WAS IN HONG KONG I SAID TO THIS WAITER, 'ARE THERE ANY CHINESE JEWS?' HE SAID, 'I DUNNO. I'LL GO AND FIND OUT.' SO HE WENT AND HE CAME BACK. HE SAID, 'NO. THERE'S ONLY APPLE JUICE, PINEAPPLE JUICE, AND ORANGE JUICE!'

Dear Kai Yin,

Thank you for your letters of the 14th instant and the contact prints of Tommy's visit to Stanley, and I have pleasure in returning them to you herewith. I think those you have picked out are the most suitable for publicity purposes, so perhaps you could let me have one of each at your convenience to my London address. Mrs. Cooper has expressed a desire for two of each of the numbers which she has written on the back of your envelope, and if you can cope with this she will be very pleased.

I imagine you will have heard about the upset on Friday night regarding Tommy's 'props'. When he arrived at his dressing room prior to his performance he was horrified to find them scattered all over the room. Apparently the waiters had taken his tables!! As you know, the reason why we went to all the trouble of arranging this room for him was so that he could set up his 'props' and then leave them under lock and key. He was most upset, to say the least, and I must ask you to ensure that no one touches his 'props' unless he is present.

In case I do not have the opportunity to see you before we leave to-day for Bangkok (Rama Hotel), I should like to express my appreciation of your charming and most courteous hospitality, and hope we may have the pleasure of meeting you again some time.

Yours sincerely,

P.S. Enclosed herewith key for Tommy's dressing room.

MIFF FERRIE.

I WENT TO HONG KONG BY PLANE ... IT'S THE ONLY WAY TO FLY!

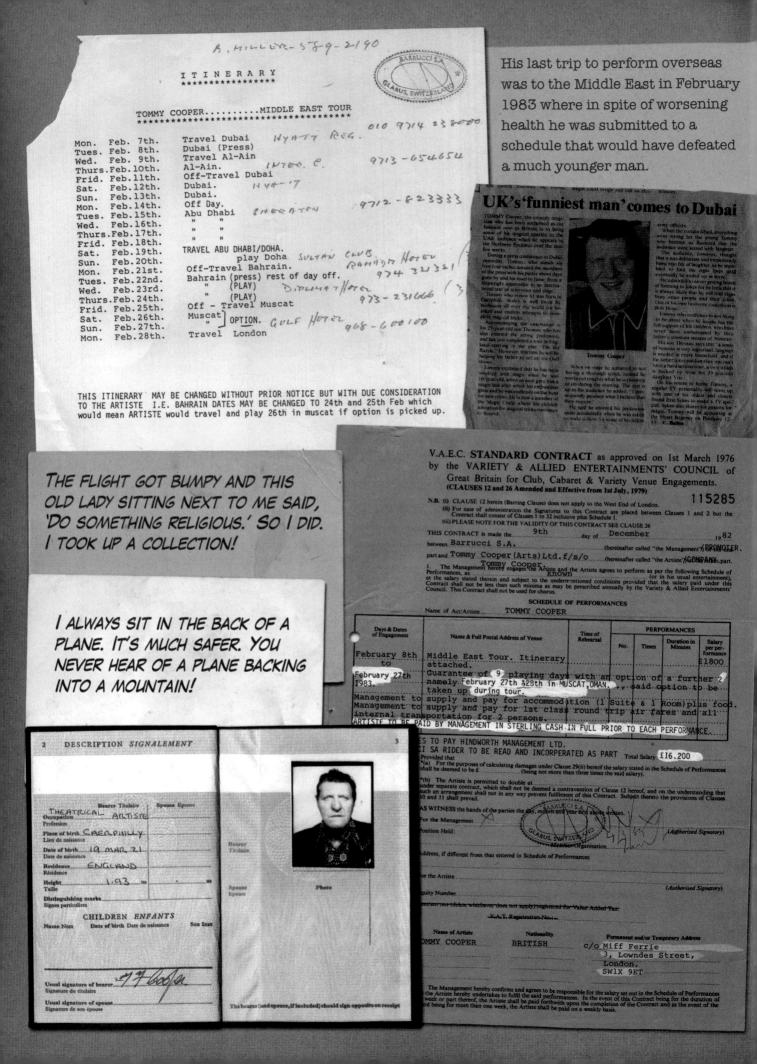

B. MILLER - 589-2190

ITINERARY
****

TOMMY COOPER.........MIDDLE EAST TOUR
****

BARRUCCI S.A.
GLARUS, SWITZERLAND

Mon. Feb. 7th.	Travel Dubai	HYATT REG.
Tues. Feb. 8th.	Dubai (Press)	010 9714 238000
Wed. Feb. 9th.	Travel Al-Ain	
Thurs. Feb. 10th.	Al-Ain	INTEC. C. 9713-654654
Fri. Feb. 11th.	Off-Travel Dubai	
Sat. Feb. 12th.	Dubai.	HYATT
Sun. Feb. 13th.	Dubai.	
Mon. Feb. 14th.	Off Day.	
Tues. Feb. 15th.	Abu Dhabi	SHERATON 9712-823333
Wed. Feb. 16th.	" "	
Thurs. Feb. 17th.	" "	
Fri. Feb. 18th.	" "	
Sat. Feb. 19th.	TRAVEL ABU DHABI/DOHA.	
	play Doha	SULTAN CLUB. RAMADA HOTEL
Sun. Feb. 20th.	Off-Travel Bahrain	974 32321
Mon. Feb. 21st.	Bahrain (press) rest of day off.	DIPLOMAT HOTEL
Tues. Feb. 22nd.	" (PLAY)	973-231666 (3
Wed. Feb. 23rd.	" (PLAY)	
Thurs. Feb. 24th.	Off - Travel Muscat	
Fri. Feb. 25th.	Muscat	OPTION. GULF HOTEL 968-600100
Sat. Feb. 26th.		
Sun. Feb. 27th.	Travel London	
Mon. Feb. 28th.		

THIS ITINERARY MAY BE CHANGED WITHOUT PRIOR NOTICE BUT WITH DUE CONSIDERATION
TO THE ARTISTE I.E. BAHRAIN DATES MAY BE CHANGED TO 24th AND 25th Feb WHICH
WOULD MEAN ARTISTE WOULD TRAVEL AND PLAY 26th IN muscat IF OPTION IS PICKED UP.

His last trip to perform overseas was to the Middle East in February 1983 where in spite of worsening health he was submitted to a schedule that would have defeated a much younger man.

UK's 'funniest man' comes to Dubai

TOMMY Cooper, the comedy magician who has been acclaimed as the funniest man in Britain, is to bring some of his magical sparkle to the UAE audience when he appears in the Northern Emirates over the next few weeks.

During a press conference in Dubai yesterday, Tommy, who stands six feet four inches amused the members of the press with his patter about days gone by and his road to fame. From a shipwright apprentice to an international star of television and stage.

Tommy, who is now 61 was born in Caerphilly, Wales, is well loved by audiences all over the world for his jokes and endless attempts to complete magical tricks.

Accompanying the entertainer is his 25-year-old son Thomas, who has also entered the acting profession, and has just completed a tour in England starring in the play "On the Razzle". However, this time he will be helping his father to set up in his Gulf shows.

Tommy explained that he has been involved with magic since he was 10-years-old, when an aunt gave him a magic box after which his enthusiasm grew and he was endlessly on the hunt for new tricks. He is now a member of the Magic Circle where his childish adoration for magical tricks continues to flourish.

Tommy Cooper

When on stage he admitted to not having a thorough script, instead he works out roughly what he is planning to do during the evening. The rest is up to the audience he added. "I consequently produce what I believe they require.

He said he entered his profession quite accidentally when he was asked to make a show for some of his fellow army officers.

When the curtain lifted, everything went wrong for the young Tommy who became so flustered that the audience were seized with laughter.

The audience, however, thought that it was deliberate and consequently burst into fits of laughter, as Tommy started to find the right lines until eventually he ended up in tears.

He admitted to never getting bored of listening to jokes for he feels that it's always likely that he will find ideas from other people and their jokes. One of his own favourite comedians is Bob Hope.

Tommy who confesses to not liking to be alone when he laughs has the full support of his children who have never been embarrassed by their father's constant stream of humour.

His son Thomas says that "a sense of humour is very important, laughter is needed in every household, and if the father is a comedian then you can't have a hard serious time, a view which is backed up from his 39-year-old daughter Viki.

On his return to home Tommy, a regular TV personality, will team up with one of his oldest and closest friend Eric Sykes to make a TV special. Sykes also shares his passion for magic. Tommy will be appearing at the Hyatt Regency on February 12-13. — C. Belbin.

THE FLIGHT GOT BUMPY AND THIS OLD LADY SITTING NEXT TO ME SAID, 'DO SOMETHING RELIGIOUS.' SO I DID. I TOOK UP A COLLECTION!

I ALWAYS SIT IN THE BACK OF A PLANE. IT'S MUCH SAFER. YOU NEVER HEAR OF A PLANE BACKING INTO A MOUNTAIN!

V.A.E.C. STANDARD CONTRACT as approved on 1st March 1976
by the **VARIETY & ALLIED ENTERTAINMENTS' COUNCIL** of
Great Britain for Club, Cabaret & Variety Venue Engagements.
(CLAUSES 12 and 26 Amended and Effective from 1st July, 1979)

115285

N.B. (i) CLAUSE 12 herein (Barring Clause) does not apply to the West End of London.
(ii) For ease of administration the Signatures to this Contract are placed between Clauses 1 and 2 but the Contract shall consist of Clauses 1 to 32 inclusive plus Schedule 1.
(iii) PLEASE NOTE FOR THE VALIDITY OF THIS CONTRACT SEE CLAUSE 26

THIS CONTRACT is made the 9th day of December 1982

between Barrucci S.A. (hereinafter called "the Management" or PROMOTER)

part and Tommy Cooper(Arts)Ltd.f/s/o (hereinafter called "the Artiste" or COMPANY r. part.
Tommy Cooper

1. The Management hereby engages the Artiste and the Artiste agrees to perform as per the following Schedule of Performances, as known (or in his usual entertainment) at the salary stated therein and subject to the undermentioned conditions provided that the salary paid under this Contract shall not be less than such minima as may be prescribed annually by the Variety & Allied Entertainments' Council. This Contract shall not be used for chorus.

SCHEDULE OF PERFORMANCES

Name of Act/Artiste TOMMY COOPER

Days & Dates of Engagement	Name & Full Postal Address of Venue	Time of Rehearsal	PERFORMANCES			
			No.	Times	Duration in Minutes	Salary per performance
February 8th to February 27th 1983.	Middle East Tour. Itinerary attached. Guarantee of 9 playing days with an option of a further 2 namely February 27th &28th in MUSCAT,OMAN. said option to be taken up during tour.					£1800

Management to supply and pay for accommodation (1 Suite & 1 Room) plus food.
Management to supply and pay for 1st class round trip air fares and all internal transportation for 2 persons.
ARTISTE TO BE PAID BY MANAGEMENT IN STERLING CASH IN FULL PRIOR TO EACH PERFORMANCE.

ES TO PAY HINDWORTH MANAGEMENT LTD.
CI SA RIDER TO BE READ AND INCORPERATED AS PART Total Salary £16.200

Provided that
*(a) For the purposes of calculating damages under Clause 29(ii) hereof the salary stated in the Schedule of Performances shall be deemed to be £............. (being not more than three times the said salary).

*(b) The Artiste is permitted to double at .... under separate contract, which shall not be deemed a contravention of Clause 12 hereof, and on the understanding that such an arrangement shall not in any way prevent fulfilment of this Contract. Subject thereto the provisions of Clauses 10 and 11 shall prevail.

AS WITNESS the hands of the parties the day, month and year first above written.
For the Management ....
Position Held: .... (Authorised Signatory)
Member Organisation
BARRUCCI S.A. GLARUS, SWITZERLAND

Address, if different from that entered in Schedule of Performances
For the Artiste ....
Equity Number .... (Authorised Signatory)

am/am not (delete whichever does not apply) registered for Value Added Tax.

V.A.T. Registration No. ....

Name of Artiste	Nationality	Permanent and/or Temporary Address
TOMMY COOPER	BRITISH	c/o Miff Ferrie 3, Lowndes Street, London. SW1X 9ET

The Management hereby confirms and agrees to be responsible for the salary set out in the Schedule of Performances the Artiste hereby undertakes to fulfil the said performances. In the event of this Contract being for the duration of week or part thereof, the Artiste shall be paid forthwith upon the completion of the Contract and in the event of for more than one week, the Artiste shall be paid on a weekly basis.

2	DESCRIPTION SIGNALEMENT		3

Bearer Titulaire / Spouse Epouse

Occupation Profession: THEATRICAL ARTISTE

Place of birth Lieu de naissance: CAERPHILLY

Date of birth Date de naissance: 19 MAR. 21

Residence Résidence: ENGLAND

Height Taille: 1.93 m

Distinguishing marks Signes particuliers

Bearer Titulaire
Spouse Epouse
Photo

CHILDREN ENFANTS

Name Nom / Date of birth Date de naissance / Sex Sexe

Usual signature of bearer
Signature du titulaire: T Cooper

Usual signature of spouse
Signature de son épouse

The bearer (and spouse, if included) should sign opposite on receipt

'HOME AT LAST!'

SHOW ME A MAN WHO COMES HOME IN THE EVENING AND IS GREETED WITH A SMILE, ENCOURAGED TO TAKE HIS SHOES OFF, HAS PILLOWS ARRANGED ALL AROUND HIM AND IS THEN SERVED A DELICIOUS MEAL, AND I'LL SHOW YOU A MAN WHO LIVES IN A JAPANESE RESTAURANT!

Underpinning Tommy's success was a versatility that embraced mime technique and juggling as well as his comedy and magic skills.

I USED TO JUGGLE PLATES WITH ONE HAND. I NEEDED THE OTHER HAND TO PICK UP THE PIECES!

He was a pretty good actor too when the comedy called for it, as the 'Hats' routine proved. However many times one saw it, it was always as if for the very first time. Like most magicians he also loved ventriloquism and rated performers like Ray Alan and the great Arthur Worsley amongst his friends.

TOMMY COOPER. Dog/vent routine.

Do persevere with this idea because I think it can be very funny once you catch onto it. It's real crazy-you to try and kid people the dog is making you talk. This way you won't have to move the dog's mouth at all.

(to audience) This dog is a marvellous ventriloquist. Well... one of us is...and his lips aren't moving. (make barking noise) See what I mean? He did that through me...watch his mouth when I bark. (bark again) Isn't that wonderful? No really. He justs sits there and out it comes through me. (gruff voice) SHUT UP. (normal voice) Hear that? Did you hear that? He told me to shut up. That's because he's so polite. You see he wants to say something and he can't bear for both of us to be talking at once. (dog voice) Pipe down. How can I use your voice when you're using it yourself? (xxxx normal voice) Go on then. (dog voice) It's about time...As I was leaving my kennel the other night a strange dog came up to me . I said do you have a family tree? He said NO; I use anybody's... (normal voice) He didn't move his lips...isn't it marvellous? (dog voice) I know a dog who never chases cats. Doesn't need to...his master's a cat burglar.. (and so on)

Get the idea? You could go on like this - this 'dog' telling the gags and you marvelling all the time. Think on it.

I KNOW A VENTRILOQUIST WHO CAN TALK FOR TEN MINUTES WITHOUT OPENING HIS MOUTH. MY WIFE CAN DO BETTER THAN THAT. SHE CAN TALK ALL DAY WITHOUT ANYTHING TO SAY!

1. Dog Gags

My wife likes to fraternize with our dog. He even sleeps with us. The other night I got bit, and up to now I'm not sure which one did it!! My wife never agrees with me. One day I yelled at the dog, and my wife said the dog was right!!

2. Dog Gags

I've also got another dog at home. He's a boxer and is so unhappy. His trunks don't fit him! He must be a bloodhound. Every time he bites me, I bleed!! Some dogs are pointers. Mine is a mudger. He's too polite to point. I got this dog for my wife. I wish I could make a swap like that every day!!

3. Dogs Gags

He said his dog was worth two. I still don't see how he could save that much!

Two dogs looking up at a parking meter. One said — What are we got to pay now!!

4. Dog Gags

I got an idea for a quiz show for Dogs. It's called — "Name That Bone"

I'VE GOT A DOG. HE'S A ONE-MAN DOG. HE ONLY BITES ME.

MY DOG IS HARMLESS REALLY. I SAY TO HIM, 'ATTACK!' AND HE HAS ONE!

The story is told of the time Tommy wrapped a chimpanzee belonging to an animal trainer friend in a blanket and went to present it to the matron of a home for unwanted children down the street! Dogs were more to Tommy's style, as seen here in shots taken in his garden and in earlier years outside his parents' bungalow just outside Southampton.

To: My Own Adorable Wife,

This is our famous dog — "Kim." Behind the dog, is that famous — "Bum Comedian" — ME! HA!!

All my love, Tommy xxxx

MY DOG TOOK A CHUNK OUT OF MY LEG THE OTHER DAY. A FRIEND OF MINE SAID, 'HAVE YOU PUT ANYTHING ON IT?' I SAID, 'NO, HE LIKED IT AS IT IS!'

Christmas was always a special time for Cooper. He first became switched onto magic with the seasonal gift of a box of magic tricks from his Aunt Lucy when he was eight years old. He once joked on television, 'Auntie, if you're watching, thank you very much for that magic set, but I still can't do the tricks!' In later years he never refused an opportunity to put on the beard of Santa Claus, often for charitable causes.

CENTRAL HALL
Box Office CHATHAM Medway 43930

COMMENCING MON. 27th DEC.
FOR ONE WEEK ONLY
Mon. to Thurs. inc. Twice Nightly 5.30 & 8.00 P.M.
Fri. 5.30 only ; Sat. 2.30, 5.30 & 8.00 P.M.

WITH
LOS ZAFIROS
PETER HUDSON + NIGEL HOPKINS
BALLET MONTPARNASSE
REG SIMPSON TRIO
A Show for All Ages!

ALL SEATS BOOKABLE IN ADVANCE
BOX OFFICE MEDWAY 43930·WEEK DAILY 10 TO 8
BALCONY £1.25, £1 : STALLS £1.25, £1, 75p each

NOW BOOKING

TVTimes Extra
CHRISTMAS WITH THE STARS

Max Bygraves, Tommy Steele,
Aimi Macdonald,
Tommy Cooper . . . all these
and many

2s

AT CHRISTMAS OUR HOME IS OPEN HOUSE TO EVERYONE – WE CAN'T AFFORD A FRONT DOOR!

HORNES are putting a touch of magic into Christmas....

HORNES
the all-round stores for men

ONE CHRISTMAS I GOT A JOB AS SANTA CLAUS IN A DEPARTMENT STORE. ONE LITTLE GIRL SAT ON MY KNEE AND SAID, 'GUESS WHAT I'VE GOT.' I SAID, 'A DOLL?' SHE SAID, 'NO.' I SAID, 'A CHRISTMAS LIST?' SHE SAID, 'NO.' I SAID, 'I GIVE UP. WHAT HAVE YOU GOT?' SHE SAID, 'CHICKENPOX!'

Here is a page featuring Tommy with some of the famous faces with whom he worked during his career. Bruce Forsyth, a longtime friend and sparring partner, was for several years the other famous client of Miff Ferrie and understood the pitfalls of working with him, as did Barry Cryer and Roger Moore from the message on their telegram. Others recognisable from the photographs are Petula Clark, Sheila Hancock, Anita Harris, Frankie Howerd, Cliff Richard and Frankie Vaughan. Arthur Askey features in a hilarious 'Me and My Shadow' routine with Tommy as his silhouetted other half.

GPO ❋ GREETINGS TELEGRAM ❋

1123 APB 10.43 HARROW T 29/30 ALLPURPOSE =

TOMMY COOPER LONDON WEEKEND STUDIOS WEMBLEY= MIDDX

= DO YOU BELIEVE IN FERRIES STOP IF SO DONT
LET HIM PUT YOU OFF GOOD LUCK TONIGHT =
ROGER MOORE AND BARRY CRYER +

I WAS AT A PARTY WITH SO MANY FAMOUS PEOPLE, I WAS THE ONLY ONE THERE I'D NEVER HEARD OF!

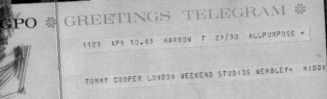

If Tommy had an empathy with one comedy colleague it was with Eric Sykes. They collaborated on several occasions, not least for the cinema in 1967 on the comic masterpiece *The Plank*, directed by Sykes, in which Cooper revealed his skills as a silent screen comedian. As a general rule, Tommy – like Benny Hill – seldom made guest appearances on other performers' television shows. With Eric he always made the exception.

ASSOCIATED LONDON FILMS Present an *Eric Sykes* film

ERIC SYKES & TOMMY COOPER in

THE PLANK 'U'

COLOUR BY TECHNICOLOR®

also starring

JIMMY EDWARDS · ROY CASTLE

Graham Stark
Stratford Johns · Jim Dale
Hattie Jacques
Jimmy Tarbuck

Written and Directed by

ERIC SYKES

Executive Producer
Beryl Vertue · Jon Penington

Produced by

MY BACK'S TERRIBLE. I WAS PLAYING PIGGYBACK WITH MY LITTLE BOY. I FELL OFF!

Tommy never wore hats in real life, but his obsession with them dates back to the age of seventeen when he was standing at a bus stop with a hat on his head. People began to laugh and snigger. Putting his feelings aside, he soon became intrigued by the comic potential of the actual article and converted embarrassment into comic gold.

SHE SAID, 'YOUR HAT IS ON THE WRONG WAY.' I SAID, 'HOW DO YOU KNOW WHICH WAY I'M GOING?'

I SAID TO THE GIRL IN THE SHOP, 'I WANT TO BUY A HAT.' SHE SAID, 'FEDORA?' I SAID, 'NO, FOR MYSELF!'

SOMEBODY GAVE ME A TEN GALLON HAT. I DIDN'T KNOW WHETHER TO WEAR IT OR SWIM IN IT!

No performance by Tommy was complete without his skilful and hilarious rendition of the classic routine with the box of hats, brought to his attention and tailored for him by Val Andrews and Freddie Sadler soon after he became famous in the mid-fifties. As Cooper told his tale in doggerel inspired by the Edwardian balladeer Robert William Service, he illustrated all the characters within his narrative by donning the appropriate headpiece dictated by the words. In time confusion reigned, but – come the end – seldom was greater comic satisfaction derived from such disarray.

TOMMY COOPER

HATS (Poem) ROUTINE

"It was New Year's Eve in Joe's Bar, a happy mob was there,

The bars and tables were crowded, lots of noise filled the air.

In the midst of all this gaeity the door banged open wide,

A torn and tattered tramp walked in, "Happy New Year, folks" he cried.

The crowd just looked at him and laughed, and some began to jeer,

But a sailor standing at the bar said, "Ship Ahoy, mate, have a beer".

I thank you, sir, the tramp replied, but me and beer are through,

"I will never touch a drop again, but I will split a bottle of rum
                                                with you."

Then up jumped a well known banker, who happened to be there,

"Throw him out" he cried, " he contaminates the air".

"Them's harsh words, sir" the sailor said; the banker said "So what",

"Them's shooting words," a cowboy said, "Are you aimin' to be shot?"

Then up jumped a soldier who was standing at the bar,

"This ain't no time to fight".."You're right" said the sailor,

And the banker said "Well, all right".

Then up jumped a woman and stared at the tramp.

"My goodness, it's Sam" she cried with fright,

And her face went white.

"Who's Sam?" a fireman asked, and the tramp then pulled out a knife,

and said.."I'm Sam" he cried, "and that painted woman is my promised
                                                bride".

"Nuts, don't make me laugh", the tramp replied, "You cannot wed that
                                                horse",

"Why not" said the fireman; the tramp replied.."We never were
                                                divorced".

"It's a lie" the woman shouted; "It's the truth" the tramp yelled out.

"Hold everything" said the sailor, "What the heck's it all about"?

"Who are you to but in" the banker said; the cowboy said "Shut up".

The soldier said "Hold it boys", and the fireman said "I'll kill that
                                                pup",

"AH..a tough guy," said a pilot, who was standing at the bar.

Then the cowboy hit the fireman, and the fireman hit the floor.

He got up straightway and said.. "I was a mug for you to fall",

TOMMY COOPER

HATS (Poem) ROUTINE (Contd.)

and then he hit her.

"By gosh" she screamed, and then the fight was free for all.

In rushed a Chinaman....in rushed a Schoolboy...A Frenchman...(Biz)

I don't know who this is...In the middle of all this fighting you

could hear the knuckles crunch....whan all of a sudden they heard a

Policeman's whistle..(Biz. followed by shound of whistle offstage)..

Then a Policeman came in and punched the whole bunch.

N.B. Tommy has his hats in a dilapitated old cardboard box. The only
other thing to be provided is the table on which the box of hats
is placed.

Tommy hit his stride on television during the latter part of the sixties and stayed one of the medium's biggest attractions until the end of his life. These pages provide a record of a few of the more surreal moments from meeting Hitler on a train to his version of 'Autumn Leaves' that helped to give him the edge over his comedy colleagues, together with some more of the jokes that have passed into comic folklore.

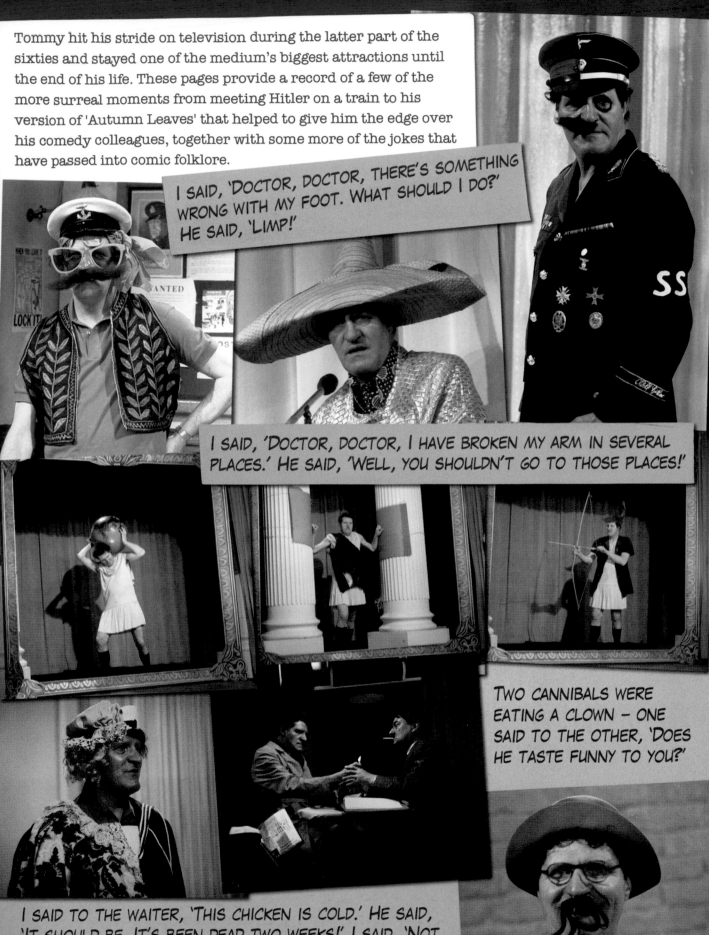

I SAID, 'DOCTOR, DOCTOR, THERE'S SOMETHING WRONG WITH MY FOOT. WHAT SHOULD I DO?' HE SAID, 'LIMP!'

I SAID, 'DOCTOR, DOCTOR, I HAVE BROKEN MY ARM IN SEVERAL PLACES.' HE SAID, 'WELL, YOU SHOULDN'T GO TO THOSE PLACES!'

TWO CANNIBALS WERE EATING A CLOWN – ONE SAID TO THE OTHER, 'DOES HE TASTE FUNNY TO YOU?'

I SAID TO THE WAITER, 'THIS CHICKEN IS COLD.' HE SAID, 'IT SHOULD BE. IT'S BEEN DEAD TWO WEEKS!' I SAID, 'NOT ONLY THAT, IT'S GOT ONE LEG SHORTER THAN THE OTHER.' HE SAID, 'WHAT DO YOU WANT TO DO? EAT IT OR DANCE WITH IT!'

I WENT IN A PUB AND HAD A PLOUGHMAN'S LUNCH. HE WASN'T HALF MAD!

I SAID, 'DOCTOR, DOCTOR, I FEEL LIKE A PAIR OF CURTAINS.' HE SAID, 'THEN PULL YOURSELF TOGETHER!'

I BACKED A HORSE TODAY – 20 TO 1. IT CAME IN 20 PAST 4!

I WAS CLEANING OUT THE ATTIC THE OTHER DAY – WITH THE WIFE – FILTHY, DIRTY, AND COVERED WITH COBWEBS – BUT SHE'S GOOD TO THE KIDS. AND I FOUND THIS OLD VIOLIN AND THIS OIL PAINTING. SO I TOOK THEM TO AN EXPERT AND HE SAID TO ME, 'WHAT YOU'VE GOT THERE – YOU'VE GOT A STRADIVARIUS AND A REMBRANDT. UNFORTUNATELY ... STRADIVARIUS WAS A TERRIBLE PAINTER AND REMBRANDT MADE ROTTEN VIOLINS!'

These later photographs show Gwen at home in Chiswick amongst her souvenirs and Tommy on one of his last holidays in Nice.

Nice

THE OTHER DAY I CAME HOME AND THE WIFE WAS CRYING HER EYES OUT. I SAID, 'WHAT ARE YOU CRYING FOR?' SHE SAID, 'I'M HOMESICK.' I SAID, 'THIS IS YOUR HOME.' SHE SAID, 'I KNOW AND I'M SICK OF IT!'

Nice

THIS FELLOW SAID TO ME YESTERDAY, 'DO YOU ALWAYS DRINK YOUR GIN NEAT?' I SAID, 'NO. AS A MATTER OF FACT, SOMETIMES I DON'T WEAR A TIE AND HAVE MY SHIRT HANGING OUT!'

These two photos are the last known to have been taken of him – at Las Palmas a few weeks before his death. He looks well and contented. It was time to sit back and truly savour the sun. Alas the longer reward for a life in which he gave so much happiness to others was not to be.

I DON'T KNOW WHAT TO GET MY WIFE FOR HER BIRTHDAY. I DON'T KNOW WHETHER TO BUY HER A BOX OF CHOCOLATES, A DIAMOND RING, A FUR COAT OR A NEW CAR. THAT'S WHAT I'LL GET HER ... A BOX OF CHOCOLATES!

I ALWAYS HAVE A WONDERFUL TIME WHEN I GO ON MY HOLIDAYS BECAUSE I HAVEN'T GOT ONE OF THOSE WIVES WHO SAYS, 'WHERE HAVE YOU BEEN? HOW MUCH HAVE YOU SPENT? WHO HAVE YOU BEEN WITH?' SHE DOESN'T SAY THAT. SHE COMES WITH ME!

Tommy died on stage during a live television performance of *Live from Her Majesty's* on the ITV network on 15th April 1984. Cause of death was later given as 'coronary occlusion due to atheroma'. Never were the contrasting masks of comedy and tragedy more indissolubly merged than they were on that night.

TEL ████████ (01) 235 9854
GRAMS) EMMEFF, LONDON, S.W.I
CABLES)

3 LOWNDES STREET,
█████████████,
LONDON, S.W. 1

MIFF FERRIE
ENTERTAINMENTS
(INCORPORATING MIFF FERRIE ORCHESTRAS)
████████████████████████████

Artiste's Name   Tommy Cooper

It is understood that Miff Ferrie Entertainments act only as Agent and is in no way responsible for any breach of Contract on the part of either the Proprietor or Artiste through whatever cause arising.

To MIFF FERRIE ENTERTAINMENTS   29th March   19 84

IN CONSIDERATION of your having procured for me (us) the undermentioned engagement(s) which I (we) hereby agree to accept through you with............London Weekend Television Ltd.,

of Television Centre, Kent House, Upper Ground, London, SEI 9LT

to appear ███████████ as   known

One night "LIVE FROM HER MAJESTY'S II" programme.

........................at..Her Majesty's Theatre.commencing.Sunday 15th April...1984...at £6,000. plus
.................................London.   (six thousand pounds)   VAT
........................at.................................commencing.......................19....at £......
........................at.................................commencing.......................19....at £......
........................at.................................commencing.......................19....at £......
........................at.................................commencing.......................19....at £......
........................at.................................commencing.......................19....at £......

I (we) hereby agree to pay you, the said Miff Ferrie Entertainments your executors, administrators or assigns, a commission of fifteen (15%)...............per centum on the salary accruing from the above-mentioned engagement(s), and on any prolongation thereof, and I (we) hereby authorise the management to deduct and pay the said commission from my (our) salary in any manner you may deem expedient. In the event of any of the above-mentioned engagement(s) not being fulfilled owing to any neglect or default on my (our) part (except from certified illness), the said commission shall notwithstanding be payable as if the engagement(s) had been wholly fulfilled.

I (we) assure you that I (we) have not entered into any engagement(s) which will debar me (us) from fulfilling the engagement(s) above referred to.

I (we) agree to pay also a like commission on the next engagement(s) with the above management if made within TWELVE months of the expiration of the said engagement.

The commission shall be payable in the event of one or any of the above engagements being transferred to another Venue.

I hereby acknowledge the receipt of a copy of this Commission Note at the time of signing the original.

Signed X ....
Permanent Address ....51, Barrowgate Rd.,
                                                W.4.

Contract No. CO6544/PJR/JPF

3 Low

LONDON WEEKEND TELEVISION
Tel: 01 - 261 3270

1. A CONTRACT incorporating the terms and conditions of the ...
between ... the Inde...
made between ... March ...
between ... whose p...
Televisio ... ondon St...
Compan ... RTS) ...
          ... es Stre...

(hereina...

WHEREAS ... engagem...
The Com ... rvices ...
████████ ... in th...
after ... " Prog...
entitl ... to ...

2. PERIOD O...

PROM ...

Rehearsa...

Studio L...
Additiona...

Approxim...

3. FEES...
(a) ...

Are...

No...
are...
add...
be...

(b) S...

(c) ...

No...

4. TIM...

7.45 Live From Her Majesty's
JIMMY TARBUCK
DONNY OSMOND
TOMMY COOPER
HOWARD KEEL
LES DENNIS
DUSTIN GEE
ADRIAN WALSH
THE THREE DEGREES
THE FLYING PICKETS
The Brian Rogers Dancers
Alyn Ainsworth and his Orchestra

Jimmy Tarbuck hosts the fifth of a series of entertainment specials from Her Majesty's Theatre in the West End of London.

See page 63
DESIGNER BILL McPHERSON
DIRECTOR
ALASDAIR MACMILLAN
PRODUCER DAVID BELL
London Weekend Television Production

G·O·W·R

The Grand Order of Water Rats
A Service of Thanksgiving for the life of
Tommy Cooper
will be held in
The Royal Parish Church of
St. Martin-in-the-Fields
Trafalgar Square, W.C.2
on
Thursday, 19th July, 1984 at 12.30 p.m.
Please bring this Ticket with you.

ST. MARTIN-IN-THE-FIELDS
Trafalgar Square, W.C.2

TOMMY COOPER
(1921-1984)

GRAND ORDER OF WATER RATS

SERVICE OF THANKSGIVING

Thursday, 19th July, 1984
12.30 p.m.

G·O·W·R

Service Conducted by
CANON EDWYN YOUNG, C.V.O.
*Former Chaplain to H.M. The Queen
and Chairman of the Actors' Church Union*

I GOT TO THINKING THE OTHER DAY — ISN'T IT FUNNY ALL THE GREAT STAGE MAGICIANS ARE DEAD? HOUDINI'S DEAD. DANTE'S DEAD. JASPER MASKELYNE'S DEAD. COME TO THINK OF IT, I'M NOT FEELING SO WELL MYSELF!

THIS FELLOW KNOCKED AT A DOOR AND SAID, 'HELLO. IS CHARLIE IN?' THE WOMAN REPLIED, 'CHARLIE DIED LAST NIGHT.' THE MAN SAID, 'HE DIDN'T SAY ANYTHING ABOUT A POT OF PAINT, DID HE?'

A rare shot of Tommy in rehearsal – serious and contemplative, as the public seldom saw him. He was wearing a similar magic cloak at the moment of his death.

Acknowledgements

In compiling this scrapbook I have drawn upon all aspects of the collection appertaining to Tommy Cooper that I have amassed over the years. That I was able to do so signals not least a large degree of thanks to Gwen Cooper and to Miff and Beatrice Ferrie. Tommy's daughter Vicky has also kindly contributed personal items to these pages, many of which have not appeared in print before. I am grateful to her and her representative, John Miles, for allowing me to continue to champion the cause of the man who made me laugh longest and loudest during my formative years and showed to me a kindness and courtesy during the times we later worked together in a manner one does not necessarily expect from one's heroes. Remarks and information written on some images – dates, description, comments – are invariably those of Tommy and Gwen Cooper themselves.

Others to whom I owe thanks for the completion of this volume are Val Andrews, Richard Anthony Baker, Eddie Bayliss, David Drummond, the team at FremantleMedia, Eddie Gay, Billy Glason, Robert Harper, Peter Hudson, Tudor Jones and the members of the Tommy Cooper Appreciation Society, Henry Lewis, Mike Maloney, Freddie Sadler, Eric Sykes, Ian Vaughan, Christopher Woodward, Audrey Worsley and Michael Worsley, not to mention the anonymous journalists and editors, photographers and artists who reported upon the Tommy Cooper story during his career. Martin Breese allowed me access to the advertisements of many of the tricks Tommy acquired from Harry Stanley's Unique Magic Studio, but sadly passed away before he could see the results of his kindness.

Images are copyright of the author's collection and the Tommy Cooper Estate. While every effort has been made to trace additional owners of copyright material produced herein, the publishers would like to apologise for any omissions and will be pleased to incorporate missing acknowledgements in future editions, provided that notification is made to them in writing.

I am indebted once again to Trevor Dolby at Preface, whose enthusiasm for my subject matches my own. The skills and patience of my managing editor, Nicola Taplin, and her colleague, Phil Brown, have been crucial to this project, as have been the promotional efforts of Rob Waddington, Andrew Sauerwine, Mathew Watterson, Chris Turner, Lee-Anne Williams and Debbie McNally.

Andy Spence has excelled himself with the design of a volume that captures so vividly the fun and personality of its subject. Without question, both Tommy and Gwen would have loved his layout at first sight. None of it would have happened without the continued encouragement of my representative, Charles Armitage, linked to the constant help of his associate, Di Evans. The loving support at all times of my wife, Sue, goes without saying.

JOHN FISHER

THIS FELLOW KNOCKED AT A DOOR AND SAID, 'HELLO. IS CHARLIE IN?' THE WOMAN REPLIED, 'CHARLIE DIED LAST NIGHT.' THE MAN SAID, 'HE DIDN'T SAY ANYTHING ABOUT A POT OF PAINT, DID HE?'

A rare shot of Tommy in rehearsal – serious and contemplative, as the public seldom saw him. He was wearing a similar magic cloak at the moment of his death.

Acknowledgements

In compiling this scrapbook I have drawn upon all aspects of the collection appertaining to Tommy Cooper that I have amassed over the years. That I was able to do so signals not least a large degree of thanks to Gwen Cooper and to Miff and Beatrice Ferrie. Tommy's daughter Vicky has also kindly contributed personal items to these pages, many of which have not appeared in print before. I am grateful to her and her representative, John Miles, for allowing me to continue to champion the cause of the man who made me laugh longest and loudest during my formative years and showed to me a kindness and courtesy during the times we later worked together in a manner one does not necessarily expect from one's heroes. Remarks and information written on some images – dates, description, comments – are invariably those of Tommy and Gwen Cooper themselves.

Others to whom I owe thanks for the completion of this volume are Val Andrews, Richard Anthony Baker, Eddie Bayliss, David Drummond, the team at FremantleMedia, Eddie Gay, Billy Glason, Robert Harper, Peter Hudson, Tudor Jones and the members of the Tommy Cooper Appreciation Society, Henry Lewis, Mike Maloney, Freddie Sadler, Eric Sykes, Ian Vaughan, Christopher Woodward, Audrey Worsley and Michael Worsley, not to mention the anonymous journalists and editors, photographers and artists who reported upon the Tommy Cooper story during his career. Martin Breese allowed me access to the advertisements of many of the tricks Tommy acquired from Harry Stanley's Unique Magic Studio, but sadly passed away before he could see the results of his kindness.

Images are copyright of the author's collection and the Tommy Cooper Estate. While every effort has been made to trace additional owners of copyright material produced herein, the publishers would like to apologise for any omissions and will be pleased to incorporate missing acknowledgements in future editions, provided that notification is made to them in writing.

I am indebted once again to Trevor Dolby at Preface, whose enthusiasm for my subject matches my own. The skills and patience of my managing editor, Nicola Taplin, and her colleague, Phil Brown, have been crucial to this project, as have been the promotional efforts of Rob Waddington, Andrew Sauerwine, Mathew Watterson, Chris Turner, Lee-Anne Williams and Debbie McNally.

Andy Spence has excelled himself with the design of a volume that captures so vividly the fun and personality of its subject. Without question, both Tommy and Gwen would have loved his layout at first sight. None of it would have happened without the continued encouragement of my representative, Charles Armitage, linked to the constant help of his associate, Di Evans. The loving support at all times of my wife, Sue, goes without saying.

JOHN FISHER